NOODLE NIGHT

Deborah Kaloper

60+ RECIPES FOR DATE NIGHTS, LAZY NIGHTS AND PARTY NIGHTS

Smith Street Books

INTRODUCTION

Forget dinosaur bones and King Tut's gold – in 2005 Chinese archaeologists discovered a perfectly preserved 4000-year-old bowl of yellow millet noodles, apparently abandoned mid-meal by an unlucky diner. The noodles had survived millennia of floods and earthquakes without even turning soggy. That's the power of a good noodle.

Like many of the world's favourite dishes, noodles have made the leap from humble peasant food to global superstar. They've travelled further than most emperors, merchants or explorers and their history reflects migration, trade and culture ... and some banging sauces.

It was ancient Chinese cooks who first looked at their ball of dough and wondered, 'What if this were longer?' They mastered the art of stretching, pulling and slicing it into a hundred theatrical strands. Even a thousand years ago late-night noodle shops hummed in Chinese cities; today every region has its own staggering array of fresh noodles, and longevity noodles (no cutting or breaking, please) are eaten for long life and prosperity at birthdays and special occasions.

From China, noodles threaded their way across the continent along trade routes, such as the Silk Road, until they gradually encircled the world.

Japan adopted them with enthusiasm and discipline in the forms of udon, soba and then, in the early 20th century, ramen. This humble street-food import is now Japan's beloved national dish, with regional variations so specific that they can start a (very polite) argument. Loud ramen slurping is never seen as rude in Japan – it's a compliment to the chef. Silence suggests indifference; inhaling with gusto signals joy. This is a country that has museums dedicated to ramen, so never doubt their commitment.

Pho was cooked up in northern Vietnam in the early 20th century. The French colonisers enjoyed beef cuts, so Vietnamese cooks would slow-simmer the leftover bones into a spiced broth and add thick rice noodles. After Vietnam was divided in 1954, pho spread through the south to become a symbol of Vietnamese cuisine.

Pad Thai is also an unexpectedly modern dish. In the 1940s Thailand's government promoted noodles during a rice shortage. Chinese noodles were stir-fried with local ingredients such as tamarind, fish sauce and peanuts – the resulting, magical, pad Thai was soon embraced as the national dish.

Spicy chilled buckwheat noodles are traditionally eaten in the northern Korean winter to balance the body. These chewy noodles in ice-cold, tangy broth became a reminder of lost homes and shared heritage in the 1950s, when refugees fled to the south during the Korean War. Today they're eaten during diplomatic events, quietly symbolising reconciliation and continuity.

And, when Chinese immigrants arrived in the US in the late 19th century, they brought their noodles but adapted them cleverly for local tastes. Fried noodles had meat and gravy stirred in to cater to American palates and chow mein ('chow' is stir-fry, 'mein' is noodles) was created. It's now possibly the world's most recognisable bowl of noodles.

Europe, in the meantime, had independently invented its own noodles. Being purists, this is a book on Asian-style noodles (for Italian pasta noodles, turn to *Pasta Night*). Italian noodles should never have 'chew' – al dente resistance, yes; but never chew. So we won't be debating whether Venetian merchant Marco Polo 'brought noodles to Italy' along the Silk Road, an urban myth that's surely made him history's most maligned delivery driver.

A watershed moment in noodle history came in Japan in August 1958, when, after months of trial, error and busy flash-frying, Momofuku Ando created the first packet of instant noodles, called Chikin Ramen. In 1971 he went on to invent Cup Noodle. If anyone is ever tempted to feel superior about instant noodles, Ando's goal was to alleviate hunger in Japan after World War II, when people were queuing in the streets for ramen. His mantra was 'peace comes when people have enough to eat', and his instant noodles became a symbol of recovery, hope and Japanese innovation.

Empires may rise and fall, but noodles endure. Today, they're equally at home in a Michelin-starred restaurant, hole-in-the-wall diner or instant cup in your office kitchen, linking cultures and quietly stretching across history, one comfortingly chewy strand at a time.

NOODLES

RAMEN NOODLES	Created in Japan for ramen soup, these noodles are made from wheat flour and kansui, an alkaline powder that gives them a yellowish colour and firm springy bite so they don't become soggy in hot broth. Ramen noodles can be thick or thin, curly or straight – but are always resilient.
UDON NOODLES	Similar to ramen noodles but much fatter, these Japanese wheat-based noodles have a chewy, comforting texture, perfect for soups and stir-fries.
SOBA (BUCKWHEAT) NOODLES	Originating in Japan, soba (Japanese for 'buckwheat') noodles have an earthy, nutty flavour. They are higher in protein and fibre than other noodles and can be gluten free. Excellent in soups, but also famously refreshing when eaten cold with a dipping sauce or in salads.
CHINESE EGG NOODLES	The workhorse of the noodle world, made with wheat flour and eggs and available in all thicknesses. With good colour and a springy, chewy consistency, egg noodles are great for wonton soups and chow mein.
RICE NOODLES	Gluten free, rice noodles come in all shapes and sizes and have a neutral flavour, so are versatile for soaking up sauces and broths. Wide, flat rice noodles are famously used in pad Thai, pad see ew and Vietnamese pho.
GLASS (CELLOPHANE) NOODLES	Starches from different local ingredients are used to make glass noodles, including mung bean (China), sweet potato (Korea and Japan), tapioca (Vietnam), pea or potato starch. Gluten-free, glass noodles are springy, glossy and chewy and turn almost transparent when added to soups.
VERMICELLI NOODLES	Defined by thickness rather than main ingredient, vermicelli noodles can be made with flour, rice or a starch such as mung bean. Thin and delicate, they are often used in spring rolls and san choy bau.
SOMEN	Very thin and pale, these Japanese noodles are made from superfine wheat flour and turn glossy and chewy when cooked. Slurping icy-cold somen is a popular way to revitalise during hot Japanese summers.
INSTANT NOODLES	Invented in 1958 to help Japan through post-war food shortages, instant noodles are now one of the world's favourite kitchen short-cuts. Discard the seasoning sachets and cook with your own flavourings instead.

KEY INGREDIENTS

BEAN SPROUTS	Both mung beans and soy beans can be sprouted and used for topping noodle dishes, adding fresh, crisp crunch.
CHUNJANG (KOREAN BLACK BEAN PASTE)	Korea's essential dark fermented black bean paste is a salty, slightly sweet but savoury staple made from soy beans and wheat. Simmered in sauces, it provides a deep umami flavour.
FISH SAUCE	A pungent, savoury liquid condiment made from fish (usually anchovies) that are salted and fermented for up to two years. Fish sauce gives umami depth to dishes.
GALANGAL	A rhizome of the ginger family with a unique taste, galangal is often used in Indonesian and Thai dishes. It is similar in appearance to ginger, but with white flesh and hot gingery–peppery pungency. Peel and then grate or finely chop before adding to dishes.
GINGER	Fresh ginger adds a punch of heat and helps cleanse and lift flavours. Cut off a knob from the larger root, peel and then grate or very finely chop before adding to dishes.
GOCHUJANG PASTE	Gochujang – red chilli paste – is an ancient Korean condiment. This sweet, salty and spicy crimson paste is made from gochugaru (red chilli flakes or powder), fermented soy beans and glutinous rice.
HOISIN SAUCE	A thick, dark, sweet and salty sauce, originating in China and made from fermented soy beans, garlic, vinegar and spices. It is known as 'seafood sauce' in Chinese, although it's vegetarian.
KATSUOBUSHI	These dried bonito flakes are an essential ingredient in Japanese dashi. Paper-thin shavings of dried smoked bonito, which look like fine wood shavings, are also used in tiny amounts as a garnish.
KECAP MANIS	Thick, sweet and darkly syrupy, this Indonesian sweet soy sauce is made by adding palm sugar to fermented soy sauce.
KIMCHI	An ancient Korean staple that's only got better with age – like most fermented foods! Traditionally made with napa cabbage and radishes, today's kimchi is fermented with chilli, giving it a signature spicy tang and aroma.

KEY INGREDIENTS

LEMONGRASS

This fragrant, tropical grass has a distinctive lemony flavour and aroma. Use the white part of the stalk only and peel off the tough outer layers. Crush the stalk with the back of your knife until it splits a little, then add to your cooking.

MIRIN

Japanese sweet rice wine with a delicate, subtle flavour, mirin creates shiny glazed sauces and provides an overall balance to dishes.

MISO

This fermented Japanese paste is made from soy beans and grains, such as rice or barley, and fermented with koji – a yeast used in sake and mirin production. There are many varieties of miso, including white and red – the ingredients and ferment time determine its colour and unique flavour.

MUSHROOMS

Dried or fresh mushrooms are used to flavour dishes. Dried shiitakes give dashi an umami lift, while fresh chewy shiitakes are more delicate. Enoki are fragile, long, thin, white mushrooms with a soft, mild flavour.

OYSTER SAUCE

This thick, dark, savoury condiment has been made in China since around 1870. It was traditionally made by boiling oysters in iron basins, then drying them by the sun or over a fire.The water was reduced to a 'blackish sauce' with seawater added. Oyster sauce today is usually made with sugar and salt and thickened with cornflour (corn starch).

PALM SUGAR (JAGGERY)

A pale brown sugar made from the sap of date palm trees, palm sugar is used in sweet and savoury dishes. The sap is boiled until it thickens to a syrup. It is sold in tins, or solidified and sold in cakes.

RICE WINE VINEGAR OR RICE VINEGAR

This mellow vinegar made from brown or white rice is milder tasting and less acidic than western vinegars.

SAKE

Japanese rice wine is one of the 'holy trinity' of essential ingredients in Japanese cooking, along with shoyu (soy sauce) and mirin. Cooking sake has a lower alcohol content than drinking sake and is less sweet than mirin.

SAMBAL OELEK

A spicy, classic Indonesian chilli paste, sambal oelek is made with fresh red chillies, vinegar and salt, and is ideal for finishing noodle dishes. The sauce (sambal) is traditionally ground with a mortar and pestle (oelek) to release flavours.

KEY INGREDIENTS

SEAWEED

Flat green kombu is vital for making dashi, the basis of most Japanese broths. Nori is mainly used for sushi but is also toasted and crumbled over ramen. Wakame, available dried, easily rehydrates for adding to ramen.

SESAME SEEDS

Black and white sesame seeds are different varieties from the same plant. Black seeds are unhulled and have a nuttier, more robust taste than hulled white seeds. Both can be toasted and sprinkled on dishes for crunch.

SHAOXING RICE WINE

This famous Chinese yellow wine is made by fermenting glutinous rice and wheat yeast. Known for its amber colour, nutty aroma and slightly sweet flavour, it's used extensively in Chinese cooking.

SHICHIMI TOGARASHI

A centuries-old Japanese spice mix used for seasoning, this blend of ground chillies, sesame seeds, orange zest, seaweed and ginger is often sprinkled over ramen.

SOY SAUCE

Created around 2200 years ago in ancient China by fermenting soy beans, roasted wheat, brine and mold, soy sauce comes in many varieties: light (saltier), dark (sweeter) and tamari (gluten free). Japanese soy sauce (shoyu) is milder and sweeter with a balanced flavour.

SRIRACHA CHILLI SAUCE

First made in 1932 in the Thai town of Si Racha (although possibly based on an ancient Cantonese recipe), sriracha chilli sauce is made from a paste of chilli peppers, vinegar, garlic, sugar and salt.

TAMARIND PUREE

This sweet-and-sour paste is made from the pulp of tamarind pods and often used in Thai cooking. It can be bought or made at home by soaking blocks of tamarind pulp in hot water, then mashing, straining and simmering to thicken.

BAS

ICS

RAMEN NOODLES

1 teaspoon kansui (sodium carbonate powder; see note)

1 teaspoon fine sea salt

220 ml (7½ fl oz) water, at room temperature

500 g (3⅓ cups) 00 flour, plus extra for dusting

Dissolve the kansui and salt in the water.

Place the flour in the bowl of a stand mixer fitted with a dough hook attachment. Mix on low speed while adding the water solution. Mix for 9–10 minutes, increasing the speed slightly towards the end, until you have a very crumbly, pebble-like dough.

Turn the dough out onto a lightly floured surface and knead for 2–3 minutes. Bring the dough together and shape into a flat disc. Cover with plastic wrap and rest in the fridge for 30–40 minutes to soften.

Lightly dust the bench again with flour. Cut the dough into six even-sized pieces. Working with one piece of dough at a time, and keeping the rest covered, roll the dough through a pasta machine on its widest setting. Fold the dough on top of itself so that it's a double layer, then pass through the rollers again.

Reduce the width of the rollers to their next setting and roll the dough through. Fold the dough onto itself again and pass through the machine a second time. Repeat this process again on the third-widest setting, doubling the dough onto itself and passing it through the machine a second time.

Now continue to pass the dough through the machine, reducing the width settings, but without folding the dough onto itself. Continue rolling until you are at the desired thickness for your noodles, dusting with a little more flour if required.

For thicker noodles, roll out the dough until it is 2 mm (⅛ in) thick and cut into noodles with the spaghetti attachment. For thin noodles, roll out the dough until it is 1.5 mm (1⁄16 in) thick, then cut into noodles with the capellini attachment.

Make the noodles the same day you intend to serve them. Cook them in a large pot of boiling salted water for 45–55 seconds. Drain well, shaking off the excess water, and divide among serving bowls. Top with your hot broth and remaining soup ingredients and slurp away!

Note: Kansui is an alkaline powder that gives the noodles their light yellow colour and chewy texture. It can be found in Asian grocery stores.

MAKES 1 LITRE (4 CUPS)

DASHI STOCK

BASICS

15 g (½ oz) kombu

15 g (½ oz) bonito flakes (katsuobushi)

Place the kombu in a large bowl, cover with 1 litre (4 cups) water and set aside in the fridge for 2–3 hours or overnight.

Transfer the liquid to a saucepan over low heat and gently heat to 80°C (175°F) on a cooking thermometer – this should take at least 20 minutes.

Simmer at this temperature for 5 minutes, then add the bonito flakes and steep for 5 minutes, keeping the temperature at 80°C (175°F).

Remove from the heat and strain through a fine-mesh strainer, discarding the solids.

Allow the stock to cool before refrigerating. It will keep in an airtight container in the fridge for up to 5 days.

MAKES ENOUGH FOR 2 BOWLS OF RAMEN

SHIO BROTH

BASICS

400 ml (13½ fl oz) chicken stock

400 ml (13½ fl oz) Dashi stock (see above)

3 tablespoons Shio tare

SHIO TARE

2 tablespoons fine sea salt

1 tablespoon boiling water

2 tablespoons sake

1 tablespoon mirin

2 teaspoons toasted sesame oil

1 teaspoon soy sauce

1 garlic clove, finely grated

To make the shio tare, place the salt in a bowl, pour the boiling water over and whisk until dissolved. Add the remaining ingredients and whisk to combine.

The tare will keep in an airtight container in the fridge for up to 5 days. It makes enough for four serves of shio ramen. Use 3 tablespoons of the shio tare per 800 ml (27 fl oz) of stock.

To make the shio broth, pour the chicken and dashi stocks into a saucepan and bring to a rapid simmer. Add 3 tablespoons of shio tare and whisk to combine.

Your hot broth is now ready to serve over your ramen noodles with your favourite toppings as desired.

TONKOTSU BROTH

800 ml (27 fl oz) Tonkotsu stock

1 × quantity of Tonkotsu tare

1½ tablespoons rendered pork fat

TONKOTSU STOCK

2 kg (4 lb 6 oz) pork thigh bones, sawn into 3 cm (1¼ in) discs by your butcher

2 pig's trotters, sawn in half by your butcher

1 onion, peeled and quartered

8 garlic cloves, peeled and smashed

TONKOTSU TARE

2 tablespoons rendered pork fat, or chicken fat or bacon fat

1½ tablespoons tahini

2 teaspoons soy sauce or Pork chashu braising liquid (page 26)

1 teaspoon mirin

1½ teaspoons sea salt

⅛ teaspoon white pepper

2 garlic cloves, finely grated

To make the tonkotsu stock, place the bones and trotters in a large stockpot and cover with water. Bring to the boil and blanch for 10–15 minutes, then drain, discarding the liquid. Rinse and scrub the bones and trotters, removing any brown-coloured bits of blood as they will discolour the broth.

Return the bones and trotters to a clean stockpot, add 6 litres (6⅓ quarts) water and bring to the boil. Skim off any impurities that rise to the surface, then cover with a lid and boil rapidly for 6 hours, topping up with extra water as needed.

Add the onion and garlic and continue to boil, covered, for a further 2–3 hours, topping up with water as needed. Continue to cook until the liquid has reduced to about 2 litres (8 cups). You should be left with a milky-white, collagen-rich thick stock.

Strain the broth, discarding the bones, onion and garlic.

Leave the stock to cool before refrigerating; it will keep in an airtight container in the fridge for up to 5 days, or in the freezer for up to 3 months. The fat on top of the stock can be skimmed off and refrigerated in a sealed container for 1 month, or frozen for up to 3 months.

To make the tonkotsu tare, whisk the ingredients in a small bowl to combine. The tare will keep in an airtight container in the fridge for up to 5 days, ready to add to your simmering tonkotsu stock.

To make the tonkotsu broth, place all the ingredients in a saucepan and bring to a simmer, whisking to combine. Serve over ramen noodles, adding your favourite toppings as desired.

MAKES 4

AJITSUKE TAMAGO

SEASONED RAMEN EGGS

4 eggs, at room temperature

125 ml (½ cup) soy sauce

60 ml (¼ cup) mirin

60 ml (¼ cup) sake

3 teaspoons caster (superfine) sugar

1 garlic clove, peeled and smashed

Place the eggs in a saucepan of boiling water and boil for 6 minutes. Drain and plunge into an ice water bath to cool for 2–3 minutes.

Meanwhile, combine the remaining ingredients in a saucepan over medium heat and simmer for 1–2 minutes, until the sugar has dissolved. Remove from the heat, transfer to a heatproof bowl and set aside to cool completely.

Peel the eggs and place them in the cooled soy sauce mixture, turning to coat them all over. Cover and refrigerate for 4–5 hours, or up to 12 hours, depending on the taste and texture desired. The longer you leave the eggs, the stronger the flavour will be, and they'll be a little firmer in texture.

Cut the eggs in half and serve with your ramen of choice. You can either discard the soy sauce mixture or use it to season your ramen.

MAKES 3

MAYAK EGGS

3 eggs

185 ml (¾ cup) Dashi broth (page 16; see Note)

185 ml (¾ cup) soy sauce

3 tablespoons brown sugar or honey

2 garlic cloves, finely chopped

1 long red chilli, finely chopped

1 spring onion (scallion), thinly sliced

1 shallot, finely chopped

2½ teaspoons toasted sesame seeds

Place the eggs in a saucepan of boiling water and boil for 6 minutes for a jammy yolk or 7 minutes for a slightly firmer yolk. Drain and plunge into an ice water bath to cool for 2–3 minutes.

While the eggs are cooling, place the remaining ingredients in a large ziplock bag. Firmly seal the bag and shake to dissolve the sugar, then set the bag in a bowl.

When the eggs have cooled completely, remove the shells and pop them into the marinade. Firmly seal the top of the bag, then swirl the liquid around the eggs.

Leave the eggs to marinate in the fridge for 3–4 hours, or overnight if you have time.

Note: You can make your own dashi broth using the recipe on page 16. Alternatively, you can buy dashi powder from Asian grocery stores and reconstitute the desired amount of broth for any of the recipes in this book.

MAKES 350 ML (12 FL OZ)

SWEET CHILLI SAUCE

BASICS

125 g (4½ oz) long red chillies, stems removed

3 teaspoons freshly minced garlic

125 ml (½ cup) rice wine vinegar

115 g (½ cup) caster (superfine) sugar

1 teaspoon light soy sauce

½ teaspoon fish sauce

½ teaspoon sea salt

2½ teaspoons cornflour (corn starch)

Roughly chop the chillies and place in a food processor, including the seeds. Add the garlic and blitz the mixture until processed into small pieces. Set aside.

Pour the vinegar and 125 ml (½ cup) water into a small saucepan. Add the sugar, soy sauce, fish sauce and salt. Bring to a rapid simmer over medium heat, whisking until the sugar has dissolved.

Stir in the blended chillies and garlic, reduce the heat and gently simmer for 4–5 minutes, for the flavours to meld.

Mix the cornflour with 2½ teaspoons water to create a slurry, then whisk it into the chilli sauce. Simmer for just a minute thicken the sauce, then remove from the heat and set aside to cool.

The sweet chilli sauce will keep in a sealed glass jar in the fridge for up to 2 weeks.

MAKES 160 ML (⅔ CUP)

NUOC CHAM DIPPING SAUCE

BASICS

2 tablespoons warm water

2 tablespoons white sugar

3 tablespoons fish sauce

3 tablespoons lime juice

1 tablespoon white vinegar

2 red bird's eye chillies, finely chopped

2 garlic cloves, finely chopped

In a small bowl, whisk together the warm water and sugar. Once the sugar has dissolved, add the remaining ingredients and mix to combine.

Taste and adjust the balance of sweet, sour and salty flavours to your liking before serving.

The dipping sauce pairs well with spring rolls, rice paper rolls, grilled pork and green mango salad.

MAKES ABOUT 125 ML (½ CUP)

MISO GINGER DRESSING

BASICS

2½ tablespoons white miso paste (shiro miso)

2½ tablespoons mirin

4 teaspoons rice wine vinegar

1½ teaspoons freshly grated ginger

1 teaspoon toasted sesame oil

1 teaspoon soy sauce

Place all the ingredients in a clean glass jar. Add 1 teaspoon water, secure the lid and shake to combine.

The dressing will keep in the fridge for up to 1 week.

MAKES ABOUT 160 ML (⅔ CUP)

TOASTED SESAME DRESSING

BASICS

45 g (scant ⅓ cup) sesame seeds

60 g (¼ cup) kewpie mayonnaise

1½ tablespoons light soy sauce

1 tablespoon rice wine vinegar

2½–3 teaspoons caster (superfine) sugar

2 teaspoons toasted sesame oil

1 teaspoon white miso paste (shiro miso)

Place a wok or frying pan over medium–high heat and add the sesame seeds. Lightly toast the seeds, stirring often, for 2–3 minutes, or until fragrant and golden.

Immediately tip the seeds into a mortar and use the pestle to grind the sesame seeds to a powder. (You can also use a spice grinder, pulsing a few times until the seeds have turned into a fine powder.)

Transfer the sesame seed powder to a bowl, add the remaining ingredients and whisk to combine. Taste and adjust the sweetness as desired.

The dressing will keep in a sealed glass container in the fridge for 5–7 days.

MAKES 125 ML (½ CUP)

PEANUT CHILLI SAUCE

BASICS

2 tablespoons peanut butter

2 tablespoons soy sauce

1½ tablespoons crushed peanuts

1½ tablespoons brown sugar

1 tablespoon rice wine vinegar

1½ teaspoons sambal oelek

1 teaspoon freshly minced garlic

squeeze of lime juice (optional)

Place all the ingredients in a bowl and whisk to combine. Taste and adjust the flavour with more sambal oelek, sugar or lime juice as desired.

Use as a dipping sauce or salad dressing.

MAKES 175 ML (6 FL OZ)

NAM JIM SAUCE

BASICS

4 garlic cloves, finely minced

4 red bird's eye chillies, finely minced

1 long red chilli, finely minced

60 ml (¼ cup) lime juice

55 g (¼ cup) caster (superfine) sugar

1½ tablespoons Thai fish sauce

1½ tablespoons finely chopped coriander (cilantro)

Place all the ingredients in a clean glass jar, secure the lid and shake until the sugar has dissolved.

The sauce will keep in the fridge for 3–4 days.

Nam jim is great with seafood and as a dipping sauce.

MAKES 200 G (7 OZ)

VIETNAMESE PICKLES

BASICS

- 150 g (5½ oz) caster (superfine) sugar
- 300 ml (10 fl oz) warm water
- 200 ml (7 fl oz) white vinegar
- 100 g (3½ oz) carrot, julienned
- 100 g (3½ oz) daikon, julienned
- 1 red bird's eye chilli, split lengthways, stem removed

Combine the sugar and warm water in a bowl and whisk together to dissolve the sugar. Allow the liquid to cool.

Add the remaining ingredients, then cover and leave to pickle in the fridge for 50–60 minutes before using.

The pickles will keep in an airtight container in the fridge for 5–6 days.

MAKES 325 ML (11 FL OZ)

CHILLI CRISP OIL

BASICS

- 25 g (¼ cup) sichuan or red chilli flakes
- 2 tablespoons crispy fried shallots (store-bought)
- 2 tablespoons crispy fried garlic (store-bought)
- 2 tablespoons sesame seeds
- 2 tablespoons crushed roasted salted peanuts
- 1 tablespoon gochugaru chilli powder
- 1 tablespoon shichimi togarashi
- 2 teaspoons white sugar
- 1 teaspoon sea salt flakes
- 1 star anise
- 250 ml (1 cup) peanut oil

Combine all the ingredients, except the peanut oil, in a heatproof bowl.

Pour the oil into a small pan and place over high heat. When the oil reaches 135°C (275°F) on a cooking thermometer, carefully pour the hot oil over the spice mixture and allow the flavours to meld for 1 minute.

Use immediately or leave to cool before storing in a sealed glass jar. The oil will keep in the fridge for 2–3 weeks.

NOOD
S

LE
OUPS

SERVES 2

TONKOTSU RAMEN WITH PORK CHASHU

NOODLE SOUPS

6 slices Chashu pork (see below)

2 portions thin Ramen noodles (page 14), cooked al dente and drained

800 ml (27 fl oz) Tonkotsu broth (page 17), simmering

20 g (¾ oz) fresh wood ear mushrooms, sliced

8 pieces fermented bamboo shoots (menma), or 8 tinned bamboo shoot slices

2 Ajitsuke tamago (page 18), halved

1 toasted nori sheet, cut into quarters

2 teaspoons thinly sliced garlic chives

PORK CHASHU

1 kg (2 lb 3 oz) boneless pork belly, skin on

250 ml (1 cup) sake

250 ml (1 cup) mirin

125 ml (½ cup) soy sauce

125 ml (½ cup) caster (superfine) sugar

4 spring onions (scallions), quartered

2 shallots, peeled and halved

6 garlic cloves, peeled and smashed

20 g (¾ oz) ginger, sliced

Preheat the oven to 135°C (275°F) fan-forced.

To make the pork chashu, roll up the pork belly with the skin on the outside. Tie up with kitchen string, at 2 cm (¾ in) intervals all along the pork.

Place the remaining ingredients and 500 ml (2 cups) water in a flameproof casserole dish and bring to the boil. Remove from the heat and add the pork.

Put the lid on and transfer to the oven. Cook for 4–5 hours, turning the pork occasionally, until completely cooked through and tender.

Remove the dish from the oven and allow the pork to cool in the braising liquid. Leave covered in the fridge overnight for maximum flavour.

To serve, remove the pork from the braising liquid and thinly slice. Reheat the strained braising liquid, add six slices of chashu pork and slowly simmer until the pork is warmed through.

Quickly and evenly divide the warm drained noodles between two soup bowls and pour the hot tonkotsu broth over the top. Finish with the mushrooms, bamboo shoots, egg halves, nori and pork chashu slices. Sprinkle over the garlic chives and serve immediately.

Notes: The strained braising liquid can be used as a marinade for Ajitsuke tamago (page 18), as a tare seasoning for Tonkotsu broth (page 17) or to flavour your ramen.

The pork chashu makes enough for eight bowls of ramen. The braising liquid and the pork will keep in separate airtight containers in the fridge for 5–6 days.

SERVES 2–3

QUICK BEEF PHO

1 small onion, halved

3 cm (1¼ in) piece of ginger, halved

1 star anise

1 cinnamon stick

2 whole cloves

2 cardamom pods

700 ml (23½ fl oz) beef stock

500 ml (2 cups) chicken stock

1 tablespoon fish sauce

2 teaspoons grated palm sugar or brown sugar

200 g (7 oz) dried flat rice stick noodles

TO SERVE

100 g (3½ oz) rib eye beef, very thinly sliced (see Note)

¼ small onion, very thinly sliced

handful of bean sprouts

handful of Vietnamese mint leaves

handful of coriander (cilantro) leaves

sliced long red chilli

sriracha chilli sauce or hot sauce

hoisin sauce

lime wedges

Heat a cast-iron frying pan over medium heat. Once the pan is hot, add the onion and ginger pieces, cut side down. Leave for a few minutes until lightly charred, adding the star anise, cinnamon, cloves and cardamom pods for the final minute to lightly toast until fragrant.

Place the charred onion, ginger and toasted spices in a saucepan. Add the beef stock, chicken stock, fish sauce and sugar and bring to the boil. Reduce the heat to low and simmer for 20–30 minutes for the flavours to develop.

When the broth has nearly finished simmering, cook the noodles according to the packet instructions. Drain, rinse and divide among soup bowls.

Strain the broth, discarding the solids, and ladle the broth over the noodles. Top with the thinly sliced raw beef (it will cook in the hot broth), onion slices, bean sprouts and plenty of fresh herbs.

Serve immediately, with sliced red chilli, chilli sauce, hoisin sauce and lime wedges on the side.

Note: Pop the beef in the freezer for 10–15 minutes to make slicing much easier.

UNI-EAGLE
SRIRACHA HOT

SERVES 2–3

JJAMPPONG

SPICY MIXED SEAFOOD NOODLE SOUP

1 tablespoon peanut oil

1 tablespoon freshly minced garlic

1 teaspoon freshly minced ginger

¼ onion, thinly sliced

½ carrot, julienned

½ zucchini (courgette), halved, then sliced on the diagonal

75 g (1 cup) thinly sliced green cabbage

6 clams, cleaned

6 mussels, cleaned and debearded

6 prawns (shrimp), peeled and deveined, tails left intact

1 baby squid tube, cut into thin rings or strips, about 1 cm (½ in) thick

600 ml (20½ fl oz) fish stock or Dashi stock (page 16)

600 ml (20½ fl oz) chicken stock

sea salt and cracked black pepper, to taste

400 g (14 oz) fresh Korean jjajangmyeon noodles

SAUCE

2 tablespoons gochujang paste

2 tablespoons gochugaru chilli powder

1 tablespoon mirin

1 tablespoon soy sauce

1 tablespoon oyster sauce

TO SERVE

sliced spring onion (scallion)

Korean chilli oil or toasted sesame oil

Place all the sauce ingredients in a bowl, whisk to combine and set aside.

In a large saucepan, warm the peanut oil over medium heat. Add the garlic and ginger and toss for 30–40 seconds, or until fragrant. Add the onion, carrot and zucchini and stir-fry for another 1–2 minutes. Toss in the cabbage and stir-fry for another minute or two, until the vegetables have softened slightly.

Add the clams, mussels, prawns, squid and the sauce, tossing to combine. Cook, stirring, for just a minute or two, then pour in the fish stock and chicken stock. Bring to the boil, then reduce the heat and simmer for 2–3 minutes, or until the vegetables are tender, all the shellfish have opened and the prawns and squid rings are beautifully cooked. Taste, then season with salt and pepper as desired.

Cook the noodles according to the packet instructions, then drain and divide among soup bowls. Ladle the spicy seafood soup on top of the noodles and finish with the spring onion and a drizzle of chilli oil or toasted sesame oil.

SERVES 4

CHINESE CHICKEN & SWEETCORN SOUP

125 g (4½ oz) dried Chinese egg noodles

1.2 litres (40 fl oz) chicken stock

1 tablespoon soy sauce

2 teaspoons shaoxing rice wine

420 g (15 oz) tinned creamed corn

150 g (1 cup) frozen corn kernels, thawed

2 teaspoons freshly minced ginger

1 teaspoon freshly minced garlic

¼ teaspoon ground turmeric (optional)

2 teaspoons cornflour (corn starch) (optional; see Note)

2 eggs, beaten (see Note)

150 g (1 cup) shredded cooked chicken

2 spring onions (scallions) or garlic chives, thinly sliced

sea salt and white pepper, to taste

TO SERVE

small handful of coriander (cilantro) leaves

toasted sesame oil

Cook the noodles according to the packet instructions. Drain, rinse and set aside.

Place the chicken stock, soy sauce and rice wine in a large saucepan. Add the creamed corn, whole corn kernels, ginger, garlic and turmeric, if using. Bring to the boil over medium–high heat, then reduce the heat to a simmer.

If using the cornflour, mix with 1 teaspoon water to make a smooth slurry, then whisk into the soup to thicken.

Remove the soup from the heat and gently whisk in the beaten egg to form egg ribbons.

Return the soup to a low simmer, add the shredded chicken, egg noodles and spring onion and heat through for another minute or so. Taste and season with salt and white pepper as desired.

Divide the soup among large bowls and serve sprinkled with coriander leaves and a drizzle of toasted sesame oil.

Note: For a thinner soup, leave out the cornflour water slurry and add an extra egg white to the beaten egg mixture.

SERVES 2

NIKU UDON

JAPANESE BEEF NOODLE SOUP

400 g (14 oz) fresh or frozen thick udon noodles

2 teaspoons caster (superfine) sugar

2 tablespoons shoyu (Japanese soy sauce)

2 tablespoons sake

2 tablespoons mirin

20 g (¾ oz) piece of ginger, julienned

200 g (7 oz) wagyu beef or rib eye, thinly sliced

1 baby bok choy, sliced

SOUP BASE

800 ml (27 fl oz) Dashi stock (page 16)

2 tablespoons shoyu

2 tablespoons mirin

TO SERVE

4 slices narutomaki (Japanese fish cake)

2 spring onions (scallions), thinly sliced

shichimi togarashi

Cook the noodles according to the packet instructions. Drain, rinse and set aside.

In a large saucepan, combine the sugar, shoyu, sake, mirin and 2 tablespoons of water. Bring to a rapid simmer, stirring to dissolve the sugar. Reduce the heat to medium, add the ginger and beef slices and cook for 3–4 minutes.

While the beef is cooking, prepare the soup base by pouring the dashi stock, shoyu and mirin into a pot and bringing to a rapid simmer. Add the bok choy and cook for a minute or two, until softened.

Divide the noodles between two soup bowls. Ladle the broth onto the noodles and top with the sliced beef mixture and bok choy.

Serve straight away, garnished with the narutomaki slices, spring onion and a sprinkling of shichimi togarashi.

SERVES 2

SHIO RAMEN WITH SPINACH, BOK CHOY & EDAMAME

1 teaspoon sea salt

95 g (⅔ cup) edamame

1 baby bok choy, halved

100 g (3½ oz) baby spinach leaves

2 portions thin Ramen noodles (page 14), cooked al dente and drained

800 ml (27 fl oz) Shio broth (page 16), simmering

2 Ajitsuke tamago (page 18), halved

TO SERVE

2 teaspoons chopped garlic chives

2 teaspoons toasted sesame seeds

toasted sesame oil

Bring a saucepan of water to the boil. Add the salt, edamame and bok choy and cook for 1 minute, then add the spinach and cook for a further 30–60 seconds, or until just wilted. Drain the blanched vegetables and plunge into an ice water bath to stop the cooking process. Once refreshed, drain again, then lightly squeeze the water from the spinach leaves. Set the vegetables aside.

Quickly and evenly divide the warm drained noodles between two soup bowls and pour the hot shio broth over the top.

Top with the blanched vegetables and the egg halves. Serve straight away, garnished with the garlic chives, sesame seeds and a drizzle of sesame oil.

QUICK CHICKEN LAKSA

800 g (1 lb 12 oz) pre-cooked hokkien noodles (vacuum packed)

2 tablespoons peanut oil

230 g (8 oz) Thai yellow curry paste (store-bought)

400 ml (13½ fl oz) coconut milk

1.2 litres (40 fl oz) chicken stock

2 makrut lime leaves

1–2 tablespoons grated palm sugar, to taste

250 g (1⅔ cups) shredded cooked chicken

8–12 fried tofu puffs, halved

1 large carrot, julienned

1 red bell pepper (capsicum), thinly sliced

80 g (2¾ oz) green beans, trimmed, halved and blanched for 2 minutes

40 ml (1¼ fl oz) lime juice

TO SERVE

2 large handfuls of bean sprouts

1 large handful of coriander (cilantro) leaves

1 long red chilli, thinly sliced

30 g (⅓ cup) crispy fried shallots (store-bought)

lime wedges

Place the noodles in a bowl of hot water and leave to refresh.

Warm the peanut oil in a large saucepan over medium heat. Add the curry paste and fry off for 1–2 minutes for the flavours to bloom, stirring now and then.

Stir in the coconut milk, chicken stock, lime leaves and palm sugar. Bring to just under a boil, then reduce the heat and simmer for 2–3 minutes.

Add the shredded chicken, tofu puffs, carrot, bell pepper and green beans. Simmer for 2–3 minutes, or until the vegetables are tender. Stir the lime juice through, then taste and adjust the flavours with more lime juice or sugar as desired.

Divide the noodles among soup bowls and ladle the laksa soup over the top. Finish with the bean sprouts, coriander, chilli and crispy fried shallots and serve with lime wedges.

SERVES 2

PRAWN & PORK WONTON NOODLE SOUP

120 g (4½ oz) or two nests of dried thick Chinese egg noodles

800 ml (27 fl oz) chicken stock

20 g (¾ oz) piece of ginger, finely julienned

1 tablespoon soy sauce

pinch of white pepper

1 baby bok choy, quartered

WONTONS

80 g (2¾ oz) minced (ground) pork

50 g (1¾ oz) cleaned raw prawns (shrimp), finely chopped

2 teaspoons finely chopped chives

1 teaspoon oyster sauce

½ teaspoon freshly grated ginger

white pepper, to season

10–12 square wonton wrappers

TO SERVE

1–2 spring onions (scallions), thinly sliced

small handful of coriander (cilantro) leaves

toasted sesame oil

sliced red chilli or Chilli crisp oil (page 23)

To make the wontons, place the pork, prawn meat, chives, oyster sauce and ginger in a bowl. Add a good pinch of salt and white pepper and mix well to combine.

Lay the wonton wrappers out on the kitchen bench. Place a generous teaspoon of the filling onto the centre of each wrapper. Lightly brush two edges of a wrapper with a little water and fold over into a triangle, enclosing the filling and pressing out the air as you seal the wonton – otherwise it may fall apart while cooking.

With the longest part of the triangle facing you, dab a little water on one of the triangle points, then wrap the wonton wrapper around to the other point and pinch to seal. Continue with the remaining filling and wrappers to make 10–12 wontons.

To make the soup, cook the noodles according to the packet instructions. Drain, rinse and divide between two soup bowls.

Meanwhile, bring the chicken stock to the boil in a pot. Reduce the heat, add the ginger, soy sauce and white pepper and leave to simmer.

Add the wontons to a large pot of boiling water and cook for 3–4 minutes, until they float to the surface. A minute before the wontons are ready, blanch the bok choy in the simmering chicken stock.

Using a slotted spoon, scoop the wontons into your noodle bowls. Ladle the hot broth over the top and add the bok choy, spring onion, coriander and a drizzle of sesame oil.

Serve immediately, with sliced red chilli or chilli crisp oil on the side.

醋

SERVES 2

MISO UDON SOUP

700 ml (23½ fl oz) vegetarian dashi stock

70 g (2½ oz) white miso paste (shiro miso)

2 teaspoons tamari or soy sauce

1 baby bok choy, sliced or halved

6 snow peas (mangetout), sliced

2 fresh shiitake mushrooms, sliced

100 g (3½ oz) firm tofu, cubed

1 teaspoon freshly grated ginger

480 g (1 lb 1 oz) frozen thick udon noodles, cooked according to the packet instructions

1 spring onion (scallion), thinly sliced

shichimi togarashi, to serve

In a large saucepan, bring the dashi stock to a gentle simmer over medium heat. Add the miso paste and whisk until incorporated. Season with the tamari and lightly whisk again.

Add the bok choy, snow peas, mushrooms, tofu and ginger. Simmer for about 5 minutes, or until the vegetables are tender.

Add the cooked noodles and spring onion to warm through.

Ladle into two soup bowls and serve with a sprinkling of shichimi togarashi.

SERVES 4

PRAWN TEMPURA UDON SOUP

vegetable oil, for deep-frying

12 large prawns (shrimp), peeled and deveined, tails left intact

800 g (1 lb 12 oz) frozen thick udon noodles, cooked according to the packet instructions

TEMPURA BATTER

15 g (½ oz) cornflour (corn starch)

75 g (2¾ oz) low-protein cake flour

125 ml (½ cup) chilled sparkling water

1 egg yolk

2 ice cubes

BROTH

1.4 litres (47 fl oz) Dashi stock (page 16)

90 ml (3 fl oz) shoyu (Japanese soy sauce)

60 ml (¼ cup) mirin

TO SERVE

12 slices narutomaki (Japanese fish cake)

3 spring onions (scallions), thinly sliced

2 tablespoons furikake

shichimi togarashi

Pour enough oil into a large saucepan to reach a depth of about 5 cm (2 in). Heat the oil to 180°C (350°F) on a cooking thermometer.

While the oil is heating, make the tempura batter. Place the ingredients in a bowl and gently mix together using chopsticks. It is okay for a few lumps to remain – resist the urge to make the batter completely smooth, as this develops the gluten and makes the batter tough, rather than light and crispy. Refrigerate the tempura batter to keep it chilled while the frying oil is heating up.

When the oil is fully heated, dip the prawns, one at a time, into the batter, shaking off any excess, and carefully lower them into the hot oil. Fry three or four prawns at a time for 1–2 minutes, just until crispy, lightly golden and cooked through. Remove and drain on a wire rack or paper towel. Continue until all the prawns have been fried.

While the prawns are frying, place the broth ingredients in a pot, whisk to combine and bring to a rapid simmer over medium–high heat.

Divide the cooked noodles among soup bowls and pour over the broth. Top with the narutomaki slices, spring onion and tempura prawns. Finish with a sprinkle of furikake and shichimi togarashi and serve straight away.

SERVES 3–4

TOM YUM GOONG

THAI HOT SOUR SOUP WITH RICE NOODLES

100 g (3½ oz) dried rice vermicelli noodles

600 ml (20½ fl oz) fish stock

600 ml (20½ fl oz) chicken stock

2 lemongrass stalks, inner tender stems only, thinly sliced

8 makrut lime leaves

3 red bird's eye chillies, halved

6 cm (2½ in) piece of galangal, sliced into 8 pieces

40 ml (1¼ fl oz) fish sauce

1 tablespoon tamarind puree

1 shallot, thinly sliced

150 g (5½ oz) cherry tomatoes, halved

80 g (2¾ oz) oyster mushrooms, sliced

16 prawns (shrimp), peeled and deveined, tails left intact

40 ml (1¼ fl oz) lime juice

1 tablespoon palm sugar or brown sugar

TO SERVE

coriander (cilantro) leaves

lime wedges

sliced red bird's eye chilli

Cook the noodles according to the packet instructions. Drain, rinse and set aside.

Place a large pot over medium heat and add the fish and chicken stocks, lemongrass, lime leaves, chilli, galangal, fish sauce and tamarind puree. Bring to the boil, then reduce the heat to low and simmer for 10–15 minutes.

Add the shallot, tomato, mushrooms and prawns to the broth. Simmer for another minute or two, until the prawns and mushrooms are just cooked through. Stir through the lime juice and sugar. Taste, then adjust the flavours to your liking, adding more sugar, lime juice and/or fish sauce.

Divide the noodles among soup bowls and ladle over the soup. Top with coriander leaves and serve with lime wedges and extra chilli.

TAO
TSIN

SERVES 2

TOM KHA GAI

THAI COCONUT CHICKEN SOUP

100 g (3½ oz) dried rice noodles

400 ml (13½ fl oz) chicken stock

400 ml (13½ fl oz) coconut milk

1 lemongrass stalk, inner tender stem only, thinly sliced

2 red bird's eye chillies, halved

3 makrut lime leaves

3 cm (1¼ in) piece of galangal, sliced

2 tablespoons fish sauce

1½ teaspoons tamarind puree

200 g (7 oz) chicken breast, thinly sliced

60 g (2 oz) button mushrooms, sliced

2 tablespoons lime juice

2 teaspoons grated palm sugar or brown sugar

TO SERVE

1 spring onion (scallion), thinly sliced

small handful of coriander (cilantro) leaves

lime wedges

Cook the noodles according to the packet instructions. Drain, rinse and set aside.

Place a large pot over medium heat and add the chicken stock, coconut milk, lemongrass, chilli, lime leaves, galangal, fish sauce and tamarind puree. Bring to the boil, then reduce the heat to low and simmer for 10 minutes.

Add the chicken and mushrooms and simmer for another 2–3 minutes, or until the chicken is cooked through. Stir through the lime juice and sugar. Taste, then adjust the flavours to your liking, adding more sugar and/or lime juice.

Divide the noodles between two soup bowls and ladle over the soup. Top with the spring onion and coriander leaves and serve with lime wedges on the side.

MIEN GA

VIETNAMESE CHICKEN SOUP WITH GLASS NOODLES

1 whole free-range chicken, about 1.5–1.7 kg (3 lb 5 oz–3 lb 12 oz)

2 teaspoons sea salt flakes

1 onion, quartered

5 cm (2 inch) piece of ginger, sliced

1 tablespoon fish sauce

300 g (10½ oz) glass noodles (mung bean vermicelli noodles)

TO SERVE

4 spring onions (scallions), thinly sliced

large handful of coriander (cilantro) leaves

3 tablespoons crispy fried shallots (store-bought)

Place the chicken in a large stockpot, cover with water, add the salt and bring to the boil. Skim off any scum or foam that rises to the surface, then reduce the heat to medium.

Add the onion, ginger and fish sauce and simmer for 50–60 minutes, or until the chicken is cooked through.

Remove the chicken from the broth and leave to cool slightly.

While the chicken is cooling, cook the noodles according to the packet instructions. Drain, rinse and set aside.

Shred the chicken meat into bite-sized pieces, discarding the carcass.

Remove the onion and ginger from the broth. Taste and add more fish sauce if desired.

Divide the noodles among soup bowls, add the shredded chicken and ladle over the hot broth. Top with the spring onion, coriander leaves and crispy fried shallots and serve.

SERVES 2

SOBA NOODLE 'OCHAZUKE'

SOBA NOODLES IN A GREEN TEA DASHI BROTH

120 g (4 oz) dried soba noodles

625 ml (2½ cups) Dashi stock (page 16), simmering

1½ teaspoons Japanese matcha powder

3 tablespoons just-boiled water

handful of baby spinach leaves

160 g (5½ oz) hot smoked wild-caught salmon, flaked

1 jammy 6-minute boiled egg, halved

1–2 spring onions (scallions), thinly sliced

2–3 cm (¾–1¼ in) piece of daikon, julienned

TO SERVE

coriander (cilantro) leaves

1 teaspoon black sesame seeds

toasted sesame oil

Cook the noodles according to the packet instructions. Drain, rinse and set aside.

Meanwhile, in a pot, bring the dashi broth to a simmer.

Sift the matcha powder into a large heatproof bowl, add the just-boiled water and whisk to a paste. Add the warmed dashi broth and whisk until completely combined.

Divide the noodles and baby spinach leaves between two soup bowls, then pour over the matcha dashi broth. Top each bowl with the salmon, half a jammy egg, the spring onion and daikon.

Serve straight away, sprinkled with coriander leaves, black sesame seeds and a drizzle of toasted sesame oil.

SERVES 3

CREAMY GOCHUJANG NOODLE SOUP

3 × 100 g (3½ oz) packets Korean instant ramen noodles, seasoning sachets discarded

2 baby bok choy, sliced lengthways

2 teaspoons peanut oil

4 teaspoons freshly minced ginger

1½ teaspoons freshly minced garlic

2 spring onions (scallions), thinly sliced, white and green parts separated

500 ml (2 cups) chicken or vegetable stock

200 ml (7 fl oz) coconut milk

3 tablespoons gochujang paste

3 tablespoons smooth peanut butter

1 tablespoon soy sauce

1 tablespoon lime juice

TO SERVE

3 Mayak eggs (page 19), halved

large handful of bean sprouts

handful of coriander (cilantro) leaves

2 teaspoons toasted sesame seeds

Korean chilli oil

lime wedges

Cook the noodles according to the packet instructions, adding the bok choy for the final 2 minutes of the cooking time. Drain, rinse and set aside.

Place a wok over medium heat and add the peanut oil. When warmed, add the ginger, garlic and white part of the spring onion. Stir-fry for 30–40 seconds or until fragrant, then add the stock and coconut milk. Cook over medium–high heat for a couple of minutes, until the soup is hot.

Meanwhile, place the gochujang paste in a bowl with the peanut butter, soy sauce and lime juice and whisk to combine.

Pour the gochujang mixture into the hot soup and whisk again. Add the cooked noodles and bok choy and warm them through.

Divide the noodles, bok choy and soup among large bowls. Finish with the egg halves, bean sprouts, coriander, spring onion greens, sesame seeds and a drizzle of Korean chilli oil, to taste. Serve immediately, with lime wedges.

STIR-
FR
NOO

IED
DLES

SERVES 2–3

DAN DAN NOODLES

SPICY SICHUAN NOODLES

STIR-FRIED NOODLES

200 g (7 oz) dried Chinese wheat noodles

1½ tablespoons peanut oil

250 g (9 oz) minced (ground) pork

2 teaspoons freshly minced garlic

1 tablespoon shaoxing rice wine

2 tablespoons hoisin sauce

1½ tablespoons light soy sauce

2 teaspoons dark soy sauce

3 tablespoons chopped ya cai (preserved mustard greens)

125 ml (½ cup) hot chicken stock

SAUCE

60 ml (¼ cup) sichuan chilli oil or Chilli crisp oil (page 23), or to taste

2 tablespoons light soy sauce

2 tablespoons Chinese sesame seed paste

1 tablespoon Chinese black vinegar

1 tablespoon peanut butter

2 teaspoons brown sugar

½ teaspoon Chinese five-spice

½ teaspoon ground sichuan pepper

TO SERVE

3 spring onions (scallions), thinly sliced

2 tablespoons crushed roasted peanuts

sichuan chilli oil or Chilli crisp oil (page 23)

Cook the noodles according to the packet instructions, then drain and set aside.

In a large bowl, whisk together all the sauce ingredients until combined. Set aside.

Place the peanut oil in a wok over high heat. When hot, stir-fry the pork for about 2 minutes, then add the garlic and cook for a further 3–4 minutes or until fragrant.

Add the rice wine and allow to cook off for 30–40 seconds, then add the hoisin sauce, soy sauces and mustard greens, tossing through to combine. Stir-fry for a further minute or so, until the pork is cooked through.

Toss the warm noodles through the sauce, adding enough of the hot chicken stock to reach your desired saucy consistency.

Divide the dan dan noodles among serving bowls and top with the pork mixture. Serve, sprinkled with the spring onion, crushed peanuts and an extra drizzle of chilli oil.

SERVES 2–4

MA YI SHANG SHU

ANTS CLIMBING A TREE

STIR-FRIED NOODLES

160 g (5½ oz) glass noodles (mung bean vermicelli noodles)

3 tablespoons vegetable or peanut oil

1½ tablespoons freshly minced ginger

3 garlic cloves, minced

1½ tablespoons doubanjiang (spicy fermented bean paste)

200 g (7 oz) minced (ground) pork

2 spring onions (scallions), thinly sliced

sichuan chilli oil (optional)

SAUCE

500 ml (2 cups) chicken stock

2 tablespoons light soy sauce

1 tablespoon shaoxing rice wine

1 tablespoon dark soy sauce

2½ teaspoons brown sugar

good pinch of white pepper

Place the noodles in a large bowl, cover with warm water and set aside for about 15 minutes to rehydrate. Drain and set aside.

Meanwhile, combine all the sauce ingredients in a bowl and whisk until the sugar has dissolved. Set aside.

Place a wok over high heat, add the oil and warm through. Toss the ginger and garlic through the oil, stirring for about 20 seconds until fragrant, but not browned. Stir in the doubanjiang and let it cook out for 20–30 seconds.

Add the pork and cook for about 3 minutes, tossing and stirring, until the pork is lightly browned and covered with the spicy paste. Pour in the sauce, stir well and bring to the boil.

Add the drained noodles and stir until completely combined. Reduce the heat to a rapid simmer and cook, stirring, for about 3 minutes, until the sauce has reduced and the noodles have absorbed almost all the liquid.

Stir through the spring onion and cook for a further minute or so, until all the liquid has been absorbed.

Divide the noodles among serving bowls and enjoy immediately, drizzled with sichuan chilli oil if you'd like some extra spicy heat.

SERVES 2–3

JAPCHAE

KOREAN STIR-FRIED SWEET POTATO NOODLES

STIR-FRIED NOODLES

120 g (4½ oz) dangmyeon (sweet potato starch noodles)

100 g (2¼ cups) baby spinach leaves

1½ tablespoons peanut or vegetable oil

½ white onion, sliced

1 carrot, julienned

½ red bell pepper (capsicum), julienned

½ yellow bell pepper (capsicum), julienned

1 teaspoon toasted sesame oil

6 fresh shiitake mushrooms, sliced

1–2 garlic cloves, minced

DRESSING

3 tablespoons soy sauce

5 teaspoons toasted sesame oil

pinch of white pepper

TO SERVE

80 g (2¾ oz) diced silken tofu (optional)

toasted sesame seeds

spring onion (scallion) greens, thinly sliced

Place the dressing ingredients in a large bowl and whisk to combine.

Cook the noodles according to the packet instructions. Drain, refresh under cold water, then drain again and place in the bowl, on top of the dressing.

Blanch the spinach in lightly salted boiling water for just a few seconds, then drain and refresh in an ice water bath to retain its vibrant green colour. Drain, squeeze out all the water, and add to the noodles.

Place a wok over high heat and add 1 tablespoon of the peanut oil. When warmed, stir-fry the onion for 1–1½ minutes, or until softened but not coloured, then add to the noodles.

Return the wok to the heat and stir-fry the carrot for a minute or so, until softened, but still a little crunchy, then add to the noodles.

Now stir-fry the red and yellow bell pepper for about a minute, until just cooked, then add the peppers to the noodles.

Return the wok to the heat. Add the sesame oil and remaining peanut oil. When warmed, stir-fry the mushrooms for 1–1½ minutes, until beginning to turn golden brown. Stir in the garlic and cook for a further 30–40 seconds, until the garlic is fragrant and lightly cooked, but not browned, and the mushrooms are perfectly cooked. Add to the noodle bowl.

Toss all the vegetables with the noodles and dressing, coating all the ingredients completely.

Divide the noodles among serving bowls and top with the tofu, if using. Serve topped with sesame seeds and spring onion.

PAD THAI NOODLES

STIR-FRIED NOODLES

150 g (5½ oz) dried pad Thai noodles or wide flat rice noodles

50 ml (1¾ fl oz) peanut oil or vegetable oil

200 g (7 oz) chicken thighs, thinly sliced

2 shallots, thinly sliced

8 prawns (shrimp), peeled and deveined, tails left intact

3 garlic cloves, minced

2 eggs, beaten

80 g (2¾ oz) firm tofu, diced

large handful of bean sprouts

2 spring onions (scallions), thinly sliced

SAUCE

2½ tablespoons grated palm sugar or brown sugar

2 tablespoons tamarind puree

2 tablespoons fish sauce

1½ tablespoons oyster sauce

1½ teaspoons dark soy sauce

TO SERVE

bean sprouts

crushed roasted unsalted peanuts

Thai chilli powder or regular chilli powder

lime wedges

Cook the noodles according to the packet instructions. Drain, rinse and set aside.

Meanwhile, in a small bowl, whisk together all the sauce ingredients. Set aside.

Add 3 tablespoons of the peanut oil to a wok set over high heat. When warmed, stir-fry the chicken for 1½–2 minutes, until almost cooked through.

Add the shallot and cook for 1 minute, then add the prawns and garlic. Stir-fry for another 2 minutes, or until the garlic is fragrant and the prawns have just changed colour and are almost cooked through.

Push the ingredients to the side of the wok. Pour in the remaining oil, followed by the beaten egg, giving it a quick scramble before tossing it together with the chicken, prawns, shallot and garlic.

Add the tofu, bean sprouts, spring onion and noodles. Pour the sauce over the noodles and quickly toss together, coating everything well in the tangy sauce.

Divide among serving plates and top with bean sprouts, peanuts and a sprinkling of chilli powder. Serve straight away, with lime wedges.

SERVES 2

MIE GORENG

INDONESIAN FRIED NOODLES

STIR-FRIED NOODLES

300 g (10½ oz) fresh egg noodles

2½ tablespoons vegetable oil

2 eggs

150 g (5½ oz) chicken thighs, thinly sliced

6 large prawns (shrimp), peeled and deveined, tails left intact

3 garlic cloves, minced

3 spring onions (scallions), white part thinly sliced, green part cut into 2 cm (¾ in) batons

150 g (2 cups) shredded napa cabbage or green cabbage

large handful of bean sprouts

SAUCE

2 tablespoons kecap manis

1 tablespoon dark soy sauce

2–3 teaspoons sriracha chilli sauce or hot chilli sauce, to taste

2 teaspoons tomato ketchup

2 teaspoons oyster sauce

1 teaspoon toasted sesame oil

1 teaspoon soy sauce

TO SERVE

1 tablespoon crispy fried shallots (store-bought)

1 long red chilli, thinly sliced

Cook the noodles according to the packet instructions. Drain, rinse and set aside.

Whisk all the sauce ingredients together in a small bowl and set aside.

Add 1 tablespoon of the oil to a wok or large frying pan set over medium–high heat. Once well heated, crack in the eggs and fry, sunny side up, until cooked to your liking. Remove the eggs to a plate and keep warm.

Return the wok to high heat and add the remaining oil. Once well heated, stir-fry the chicken for about 2 minutes, until almost cooked through. Add the prawns, garlic and white part of the spring onion. Cook for a further minute or so, tossing to combine, until the garlic is fragrant and the prawns are almost cooked through.

Add the cabbage and spring onion greens, along with the sauce and cooked noodles. Toss and stir quickly for a further minute or two, until the cabbage softens slightly and all the ingredients are well coated in the sauce.

Quickly toss the bean sprouts through, then divide the saucy noodles between two plates. Top each plate with a fried egg, a sprinkling of crispy fried shallots and sliced chilli and enjoy immediately.

UNI-EAGLE
SRIRACHA HOT
CHILI SAUCE

SERVES 2–3

PAD SEE EW

STIR-FRIED SOY SAUCE NOODLES

STIR-FRIED NOODLES

200 g (7 oz) dried pad Thai noodles or wide flat rice noodles

300 g (10½ oz) chicken thighs, thinly sliced

3 tablespoons Thai black soy sauce

1½ teaspoons toasted sesame oil

½ teaspoon white pepper

60 ml (¼ cup) peanut oil

2 eggs, beaten

5–6 stems Chinese broccoli (gai lan), sliced

4 garlic cloves, minced

SAUCE

2 tablespoons Thai black soy sauce

1 tablespoon soy sauce

1 tablespoon oyster sauce

1 tablespoon kecap manis or sweet soy sauce

1 teaspoon nam prik pao (Thai chilli paste with soybean oil)

CHILLI VINEGAR

2 red bird's eye chillies, thinly sliced

60 ml (¼ cup) white vinegar

Cook the noodles according to the packet instructions. Drain, rinse and set aside.

Meanwhile, place the chicken in a bowl with the soy sauce, sesame oil and white pepper, tossing to coat.

In a small bowl, whisk together all the sauce ingredients with 1 tablespoon water until combined. In another small bowl, combine the chilli vinegar ingredients. Set them both aside.

Heat a wok over high heat and add 2 tablespoons of the peanut oil. When warmed, stir-fry the chicken for a couple of minutes, until mostly cooked through. Push the chicken to the side of the wok and add the beaten egg, stirring until scrambled. Remove the chicken and the scrambled egg to a bowl or plate and set aside.

Heat the remaining peanut oil in the wok. Add the Chinese broccoli and garlic and stir-fry for a minute or two, until the broccoli is tender and the garlic is fragrant. Toss the cooked noodles through.

Spread the noodles out over the base of the wok. Allow to sit and slightly char for about 30 seconds, then toss the noodles and leave to char for another 30 seconds on the other side.

Toss the sauce through the noodles, coating well. Return the chicken and scrambled egg to the wok and toss everything together until combined and the chicken is cooked through.

Serve straight away, with the chilli vinegar on the side.

SERVES 4

SINGAPORE NOODLES

STIR-FRIED NOODLES

200 g (7 oz) dried rice vermicelli noodles

50 ml (1¾ fl oz) vegetable oil

3 eggs, beaten

16 prawns (shrimp), peeled and deveined, tails left intact

½ onion, thinly sliced

½ carrot, julienned

3 garlic cloves, minced

½ red bell pepper (capsicum), thinly sliced

200 g (2⅔ cups) thinly shredded green cabbage

200 g (7 oz) char siu (Chinese barbecued pork), sliced

3 spring onions (scallions), sliced into batons

SAUCE

1½ tablespoons soy sauce

1 tablespoon oyster sauce

1 tablespoon shaoxing rice wine

1½ tablespoons mild yellow curry powder

½ teaspoon sugar

Cook the noodles according to the packet instructions. Drain, rinse and set aside.

Meanwhile, place the sauce ingredients in a small bowl and whisk to combine.

Place a large wok over medium heat and add 1½ teaspoons of the vegetable oil. When warmed, add the beaten egg and lightly scramble for a minute or so, until cooked. Remove to a bowl and set aside.

Heat another 1½ teaspoons oil in the wok, then stir-fry the prawns for about 2 minutes, or until just cooked. Remove from the pan and set aside.

Heat the remaining oil in the wok and stir-fry the onion and carrot for 1 minute, then add the garlic and cook for a further minute, until fragrant and lightly coloured. Add the bell pepper and cabbage and quickly stir-fry, tossing for 1–2 minutes, until the vegetables are just beginning to soften.

Toss in the char siu pork to warm through, then return the prawns and scrambled egg to the wok. Add the noodles, pour over the sauce and toss to combine.

Finish the dish by adding the spring onion and giving it all a good final toss to mix together.

Divide among serving bowls and enjoy straight away.

SERVES 2

PAD KEE MAO

DRUNKEN NOODLES

STIR-FRIED NOODLES

200 g (7 oz) dried pad Thai noodles or wide flat rice noodles

2 tablespoons vegetable oil

300 g (10½ oz) chicken thighs, thinly sliced

2 large shallots, sliced

4 garlic cloves, minced

2–3 red bird's eye chillies, finely chopped

90 g (½ cup) baby corn, halved lengthways

5 stems Chinese broccoli (gai lan), thinly sliced

large handful of Thai basil leaves

SAUCE

2 tablespoons oyster sauce

1½ tablespoons fish sauce

1½ tablespoons dark soy sauce

2 teaspoons light soy sauce

2 teaspoons sugar

¼ teaspoon white pepper

TO SERVE

lime wedges

sliced red bird's eye chilli

Cook the noodles according to the packet instructions. Drain, rinse and set aside.

In a small bowl, whisk together the sauce ingredients until well combined and the sugar has dissolved.

Place a wok over high heat and add the vegetable oil. When warmed, add the chicken and stir-fry for about 2 minutes, until almost cooked through. Add the shallot and cook for 1 minute, or until starting to soften, then add the garlic and chilli, tossing and stirring for about 30 seconds until fragrant.

Toss the baby corn and Chinese broccoli through and cook for a minute or two, or until just tender.

Pour the sauce over the chicken and vegetable mixture and add the noodles. Toss everything together and cook for a further minute, warming the noodles through.

Remove from the heat, add the Thai basil leaves and give the noodles a final toss, coating everything well in the sauce.

Serve immediately, with lime wedges and sliced red chilli.

SERVES 2

LORT CHA

CAMBODIAN STIR-FRIED RICE PIN NOODLES

STIR-FRIED NOODLES

200 g (7 oz) pork tenderloin, thinly sliced

400 g (14 oz) fresh rice pin noodles (see Note)

5–6 stems Chinese broccoli (gai lan), stalks sliced into thirds

2 tablespoons peanut oil or vegetable oil

3 teaspoons finely chopped garlic

large handful of bean sprouts

½ cup garlic chives, cut into batons

MARINADE

1½ teaspoons oyster sauce

1 teaspoon kecap manis or sweet soy sauce

1 teaspoon soy sauce

1 teaspoon fish sauce

SAUCE

2 tablespoons oyster sauce

1 tablespoon fish sauce

1 tablespoon dark soy sauce

1 teaspoon light soy sauce

½ teaspoon grated palm sugar or brown sugar

TO SERVE

2 crispy fried eggs

chilli oil

Sweet chilli sauce (page 20)

In a bowl, whisk together the marinade ingredients. Add the sliced pork and toss to coat, then leave to marinate for 15 minutes.

Meanwhile, cook the noodles according to the packet instructions. Drain, rinse and set aside.

Blanch the Chinese broccoli in a pan of salted boiling water for 1 minute. Drain, then refresh under cold running water and set aside.

Whisk together the sauce ingredients in a small bowl and set aside.

Heat the peanut oil in a wok over medium heat. Add the garlic and toss for 30–40 seconds, until fragrant. Add the marinated pork and stir-fry for a few minutes, until just cooked through.

Toss through the blanched Chinese broccoli, then add the sauce, noodles, bean sprouts and garlic chives, tossing well to combine and coat the noodles in the sauce.

Divide the lort cha between two serving bowls, top each with a crispy fried egg and a drizzle of chilli oil, and serve with sweet chilli sauce on the side.

Note: Rice pin noodles are short, plump noodles with tapered ends that are common in Cambodian cuisine. You can find them in Asian grocery stores or online.

SERVES 2

PANCIT

FILIPINO STIR-FRIED RICE NOODLES

STIR-FRIED NOODLES

2 tablespoons peanut oil or vegetable oil

100 g (3½ oz) pork loin, thinly sliced

150 g (5½ oz) chicken thighs, thinly sliced

½ onion, thinly sliced

3 garlic cloves, finely chopped

150 g (2 cups) shredded green cabbage

1 carrot, julienned

2 spring onions (scallions), white and green parts separated, thinly sliced

100 g (3½ oz) dried rice vermicelli noodles

calamansi, lemon or lime wedges, to serve

SAUCE

435 ml (1¾ cups) chicken stock

2 tablespoons soy sauce

1 tablespoon oyster sauce

1½ teaspoons dark soy sauce

1 teaspoon caster (superfine) sugar

¼ teaspoon cracked black pepper, or to taste

In a bowl, whisk together the sauce ingredients until combined. Set aside.

Place a wok over medium heat and add 1½ teaspoons of the oil. When warmed through, quickly stir-fry the pork until seared. Remove to a bowl and set aside.

Add another 1½ teaspoons of oil to the wok. Once heated, quickly stir-fry the chicken until seared. Remove to the bowl with the pork.

Heat the remaining oil in the wok. Stir-fry the onion for about 1 minute, then add the garlic and cook for a further 30 seconds, until fragrant. Toss in the cabbage, carrot and white part of the spring onion and stir-fry for about 1½ minutes, or until the vegetables are just beginning to soften.

Return the seared pork and chicken to the wok, toss the sauce through and bring to the boil.

Add the noodles to the wok, stirring to coat in the sauce. Cook, stirring now and then, for 4–5 minutes, or until the noodles are tender.

Toss the spring onion greens through the noodles and serve with calamansi, lemon or lime wedges.

SERVES 4

CHILLI PAN MEE

MALAYSIAN CHEWY FLAT NOODLES

STIR-FRIED NOODLES

400 g (14 oz) dried pan mee noodles

1 teaspoon toasted sesame oil

3 tablespoons peanut oil

4 fresh shiitake mushrooms, sliced

4 garlic cloves, minced

350 g (12½ oz) minced (ground) pork

50 ml (1¾ fl oz) dark soy sauce

1½ tablespoons kecap manis

1 tablespoon oyster sauce

1½ teaspoons white sugar

¼ teaspoon white pepper

125 ml (½ cup) chicken stock

1 teaspoon cornflour (corn starch)

CHILLI SHRIMP SAMBAL

20 g (¾ oz) small dried shrimp

18 dried long red chillies

3 shallots, roughly chopped

4 garlic cloves, chopped

2 red bird's eye chillies, stems removed

2 long red chillies

60 ml (¼ cup) vegetable oil

1 teaspoon white sugar

1 teaspoon sea salt

CRISPY IKAN BILIS

125 ml (½ cup) peanut oil

60 g (2 oz) dried anchovies

TO SERVE

2 baby bok choy, halved and blanched

4 poached eggs

To make the chilli shrimp sambal, place the dried shrimp and dried chillies in separate bowls, cover with warm water and leave to rehydrate for about 20 minutes.

Drain the shrimp and add to a small food processor, along with the shallot and garlic. Blitz until well chopped, then transfer to a bowl.

Drain the rehydrated chillies, roughly chop and add to the food processor with the fresh chillies. Blitz together into a paste, adding a tablespoon of water if needed. Set aside.

Add the oil to a wok set over medium heat. Add the shrimp mixture and stir-fry for about 3 minutes, then add the chilli mixture. Toss to combine and stir-fry for 3–4 minutes. Reduce the heat to low. Cook the chilli paste for 25–30 minutes, stirring often, until deep red and thickened. Stir through the sugar and salt during the last minute of cooking.

The sambal will keep in an airtight container in the fridge for 4–5 days.

To prepare the ikan bilis, heat the peanut oil in a small pan over high heat and fry the dried anchovies for a couple of minutes, stirring now and then, until golden and crispy. Drain on paper towel and set aside.

Cook the noodles according to the packet instructions. Drain, drizzle with toasted sesame oil and set aside.

Place a wok over medium–high heat. Add the peanut oil and stir-fry the mushrooms for 1–2 minutes, then add the garlic and cook for 30–40 seconds, until fragrant and lightly golden. Add the pork and brown for 2 minutes, breaking up the meat with a wooden spoon. Stir in the dark soy sauce, kecap manis, oyster sauce, sugar and pepper, then stir-fry for another 2 minutes. Stir in the stock and simmer for 4–6 minutes, to allow the pork to absorb some of the liquid.

Combine the cornflour and 1 tablespoon of water in a small bowl, stirring to make a smooth slurry. Add the slurry to the pork mixture and cook for a final minute until thickened.

Divide the noodles among serving bowls. Top with the pork mixture, a spoonful of chilli shrimp sambal, a blanched bok choy half, poached egg and some crispy fried ikan bilis. Serve straight away.

SERVES 2–3

BEEF YAKI UDON

STIR-FRIED NOODLES

400 g (14 oz) frozen udon noodles (or pre-cooked, vacuum-packed udon noodles)

200 g (7 oz) beef rib eye, wagyu or sirloin, very thinly sliced

pinch of sea salt

pinch of cracked black pepper

1½ tablespoons vegetable oil

1 teaspoon toasted sesame oil

½ onion, thinly sliced

2 garlic cloves, minced

150 g (2 cups) thinly sliced wombok (Chinese cabbage)

½ carrot, julienned

3 fresh shiitake mushrooms, sliced

50 g (1¾ oz) snow peas (mangetout), trimmed and sliced

SAUCE

1½ tablespoons light soy sauce

1 tablespoon dark soy sauce

1 tablespoon oyster sauce

1 tablespoon sake

2 teaspoons toasted sesame oil

2 teaspoons mirin

TO SERVE

sliced spring onion (scallion) greens

bonito flakes (katsuobushi) or toasted sesame seeds

benishoga (red pickled ginger)

Place all the sauce ingredients in a bowl and whisk to combine. Set aside.

Cook the noodles according to the packet instructions. Drain, rinse and set aside.

While the noodles are cooking, season the beef slices with the salt and pepper.

Add the vegetable oil and sesame oil to a wok set over high heat. When hot, sear the beef for about 30 seconds on each side, until almost cooked. Remove to a bowl.

Add the onion to the wok and stir-fry for about 2 minutes, then add the garlic, tossing for about 30 seconds until fragrant. Add the cabbage, carrot, mushrooms and snow peas. Cook, tossing, for about 3 minutes, or until the vegetables are just beginning to soften.

Return the beef to the wok and add the noodles. Pour over the sauce and toss thoroughly to combine, coating all the ingredients well.

Divide the noodles among serving bowls. Scatter with spring onion greens and either bonito flakes or toasted sesame seeds. Serve hot, with a side of benishoga.

SERVES 2

EGG NOODLES WITH PIPIS & XO SAUCE

STIR-FRIED NOODLES

300 g (10½ oz) fresh thin egg noodles

1½ tablespoons neutral-flavoured oil

3 shallots, thinly sliced

1 tablespoon freshly minced ginger

3 garlic cloves, minced

2 tablespoons XO sauce

1½ tablespoons soy sauce

1½ tablespoons rice wine vinegar

600 g (1 lb 5 oz) pipis or small clams, cleaned and rinsed in cold water

handful of chopped coriander (cilantro)

handful of thinly sliced spring onion (scallion)

thinly sliced long red chilli, to serve (optional)

Cook the noodles according to the packet instructions. Drain, rinse and set aside.

Add the oil to a large frying pan with a lid and set over medium heat. When warmed, stir-fry the shallot, ginger and garlic for 1–1½ minutes, until lightly golden and fragrant. Add the XO sauce, soy sauce and rice wine vinegar. Toss and stir-fry for another 1½–2 minutes.

Stir in the pipis, coating them in the sauce. Increase the heat sightly, then cover and cook for 2–4 minutes, or until the pipis have opened. Discard any pipis that have not opened.

Add the noodles and toss everything together until well coated in the sauce. Lastly, add the coriander and quickly toss it through.

Divide the saucy noodles and pipis between two serving bowls, scatter with thinly sliced spring onion and red chilli, if using, and serve.

SERVES 3–4

JJAJANGMYEON

KOREAN BLACK BEAN NOODLES

STIR-FRIED NOODLES

60 ml (¼ cup) peanut oil

120 g (4½ oz) onion, diced

3 fresh shiitake mushrooms, sliced

1 teaspoon freshly minced garlic

1 teaspoon freshly minced ginger

1 carrot, julienned

½ zucchini (courgette), diced

100 g (1⅓ cups) chopped green cabbage

60 ml (¼ cup) chunjang (Korean black bean paste)

300 ml (10 fl oz) vegetable stock

300 g (10½ oz) dried Korean wheat noodles

SAUCE

1 tablespoon cornflour (corn starch)

1 tablespoon sugar

1 tablespoon oyster sauce

TO SERVE

1 Persian (short) cucumber, julienned

2 spring onions (scallions), thinly sliced

2 teaspoons toasted sesame seeds

Add half the peanut oil to a wok set over medium heat. When warmed, stir-fry the onion for 1 minute, then add the mushrooms. Cook together for another minute or two, then add the garlic and ginger and stir-fry for a further 30–40 seconds, until fragrant.

Toss in the carrot, zucchini and cabbage and stir-fry for another 1–2 minutes, until the vegetables are just starting to soften.

Push the vegetables to the side of the pan and pour in the remaining peanut oil. When hot, fry off the chunjang for 1–1½ minutes, then mix it in with the vegetables, tossing to combine.

Stir in the vegetable stock and bring to the boil. Allow the stock to bubble away at a rapid simmer for about 4 minutes, until the vegetables are tender. Reduce the heat to low.

Quickly combine all the sauce ingredients, along with 2 tablespoons water, then add to the wok and stir it through the vegetables. Cook for a further 2–3 minutes to thicken the sauce.

While the sauce is bubbling away, cook the noodles according to the packet instructions. Drain the noodles and divide among serving bowls.

Spoon the saucy vegetables over the noodles, top with the cucumber, spring onion and toasted sesame seeds and serve.

SERVES 2

HOME-STYLE CHINESE TOMATO EGG NOODLES

STIR-FRIED NOODLES

100 g (3½ oz) dried scissor-cut noodles

2 tablespoons peanut or vegetable oil

¼ onion, sliced

1 teaspoon freshly minced garlic

1 teaspoon freshly minced ginger

280 g (10 oz) tomatoes, chopped

1–2 tablespoons soy sauce

3 large eggs

pinch of sea salt

pinch of white pepper

TO SERVE

1 spring onion (scallion), thinly sliced

toasted sesame oil

Cook the noodles according to the packet instructions. Drain, rinse and set aside.

While the noodles are cooking, add 1 tablespoon of the oil to a wok or frying pan set over medium–high heat. When warmed, stir-fry the onion for 2–3 minutes, or until beginning to soften. Toss in the garlic and ginger and cook for 30–40 seconds, or until fragrant.

Stir in the chopped tomato and simmer rapidly for 4–5 minutes, breaking it down with a wooden spoon. You want the tomato to be cooked and saucy, but still retaining a chunky texture.

Reduce the heat to low. Stir in 1 tablespoon of the soy sauce and 1–2 tablespoons of water if the tomato mixture looks dry. Taste and add a little more soy sauce if you like.

Meanwhile, set another pan on the stove over medium–high heat. Add the remaining 1 tablespoon of oil and warm through. Beat the eggs in a bowl and season well with the salt and white pepper. Pour the egg into the pan and scramble for a minute or so, until just cooked.

Stir the scrambled egg through the tomato mixture. Add the noodles and toss to combine and warm through.

Divide between two serving plates and serve sprinkled with the spring onion and a drizzle of toasted sesame oil.

COLD
NOO

DLES

SERVES 4

THAI BEEF NOODLE SALAD

COLD NOODLES

600 g (1 lb 5 oz) sirloin steak, 1 cm (½ inch) thick

1 teaspoon sesame oil

100 g (3½ oz) dried vermicelli rice noodles

200 g (7 oz) cherry tomatoes, halved

3 shallots, thinly sliced

1 Persian (short) cucumber, halved and sliced

large handful each of Thai basil, mint and coriander (cilantro) leaves, torn or roughly chopped

1 tablespoon toasted glutinous rice powder (see Notes)

DRESSING

1 small lemongrass stalk, inner tender stem only, finely minced

2 garlic cloves, finely minced

2 red bird's eye chillies, thinly sliced

60 ml (¼ cup) lime juice

3 tablespoons Thai fish sauce

2 tablespoons grated palm sugar or brown sugar

TO SERVE

crushed roasted salted peanuts

lime wedges

About 30 minutes before cooking, remove the steak from the fridge and allow it to come to cool room temperature. Season the steak well with salt and pepper, then drizzle with the sesame oil.

Heat a chargrill pan or cast-iron frying pan over high heat. When hot, sear the steak for 2–2½ minutes on each side, or until cooked to your liking. Transfer to a plate, loosely cover with foil and leave to rest for about 6 minutes.

While the steak is resting, cook the noodles according to the packet instructions. Drain, rinse and drain again, then spread the noodles over a large serving plate.

In a small bowl, whisk together the dressing ingredients.

To assemble the salad, arrange the cherry tomato, shallot, cucumber and herbs over the noodles. Sprinkle with the glutinous rice powder. Thinly slice the rested beef across the grain and arrange over the salad.

Drizzle the dressing over the salad, sprinkle with crushed peanuts and serve with lime wedges.

Notes: Instead of making the dressing, you could use Nam jim sauce (page 22) to dress the noodles.

Glutinous rice powder is available from Asian grocery stores.

SERVES 2

YUM WOON SEN

THAI GLASS NOODLE SALAD

COLD NOODLES

80–100 g (2¾–3½ oz) glass noodles (mung bean vermicelli noodles)

8 large prawns (shrimp), peeled and deveined, tails left intact

125 g (4½ oz) minced (ground) pork

1 tablespoon Thai fish sauce

100 g (3½ oz) cherry tomatoes, halved

small handful of Chinese celery leaves (or regular celery leaves)

2 shallots, thinly sliced

50 g (⅓ cup) roasted peanuts, crushed or finely chopped

handful of coriander (cilantro) leaves

DRESSING

1 tablespoon dried shrimp

3 tablespoons lime juice

2½ tablespoons fish sauce

2 tablespoons caster (superfine) sugar

2 garlic cloves, chopped

1–2 red bird's eye chillies, seeds removed if desired

1 coriander (cilantro) root, cleaned and chopped

TO SERVE

lime wedges

thinly sliced red bird's eye chilli

To make the dressing, place the dried shrimp in a small bowl, cover with boiling water and soak for 10–15 minutes. Once rehydrated, drain the shrimp, discarding the water. Place in a food processor, add the remaining dressing ingredients and blitz to combine. Taste and adjust the balance of sweet, sour and salty flavours as desired.

Cook the noodles according to the packet instructions. Drain, rinse under cold water and drain again. Set aside in a salad bowl.

Bring a large saucepan of water to the boil, add the prawns and blanch for about 1 minute, or until pink and just cooked through. Remove the prawns using a slotted spoon and add to the noodles in the bowl.

Drain almost all the water from the pan, leaving about 2.5–5 cm (1–2 in) of the cooking water in the pan. Add the pork and fish sauce and cook for 2–3 minutes, breaking up the pork with a wooden spoon. When the pork is cooked through, drain well and add to the noodles.

Toss the cherry tomato, celery leaves, shallot, peanuts and coriander leaves through the noodles. Pour the dressing over the salad and mix well to combine.

Serve with lime wedges and extra chilli as desired.

SERVES 2

BUN THIT NUONG

VIETNAMESE GRILLED PORK & VERMICELLI SALAD

COLD NOODLES

300 g (10½ oz) pork fillet, sliced about 5 mm (¼ in) thick

1 tablespoon peanut oil or vegetable oil, for grilling

MARINADE

1 lemongrass stalk, inner tender stem only, very thinly sliced

1 shallot, finely chopped

2 teaspoons freshly minced garlic

1 tablespoon peanut oil

1 tablespoon fish sauce

1 tablespoon soy sauce

1 tablespoon brown sugar

1 tablespoon kecap manis

½ teaspoon ground black pepper

VERMICELLI SALAD

100 g (3½ oz) dried rice vermicelli noodles, cooked according to the packet instructions

4–6 large iceberg lettuce leaves, roughly chopped

½ Persian (short) cucumber, julienned

handful of Vietnamese mint leaves

handful of coriander (cilantro) leaves

handful of bean sprouts

TO SERVE

Vietnamese pickles (page 23)

2 tablespoons crushed roasted peanuts

lime wedges

Nuoc cham dipping sauce (page 20)

Mix the marinade ingredients together in a bowl. Add the pork and toss to coat in the marinade. Cover and leave in the fridge for 3–4 hours, or even overnight.

Just before serving, assemble all the vermicelli salad ingredients and divide between two serving bowls or plates.

Heat and lightly oil a barbecue grill or a chargrill pan. Once hot, cook the pork over high heat for about 2 minutes each side, or until lightly charred, caramelised, cooked through and juicy.

Arrange the pork over the salad. Scatter with Vietnamese pickles and peanuts and serve immediately, with lime wedges and nuoc cham dipping sauce for drizzling over.

SOBA NOODLE SALAD

180 g (6½ oz) dried soba noodles

150 g (5½ oz) frozen shelled edamame

60 g (2 oz) sugar snap peas, trimmed and sliced

1 Persian (short) cucumber, thinly sliced

2 radishes, thinly sliced

2 spring onions (scallions), thinly sliced

½ avocado, diced

2 teaspoons freshly grated ginger, or 20 g (¾ oz) pickled sushi ginger (amazu shoga), thinly sliced

TO SERVE

Toasted sesame dressing (page 21)

1 teaspoon toasted sesame seeds

coriander (cilantro) leaves

Cook the soba noodles according to the packet instructions. During the final 3 minutes of cooking, add the edamame and sugar snap peas to blanch in the boiling water.

When the noodles are cooked, drain the noodles and vegetables, rinse well, then plunge into an ice water bath to stop the cooking process. Allow to chill for a few minutes, then drain well again.

Place the noodles and vegetables in a mixing bowl. Add the cucumber, radish, spring onion, avocado and ginger.

Drizzle the noodles with toasted sesame dressing and toss to combine. Sprinkle the sesame seeds and coriander leaves on top and serve.

COLD SESAME NOODLES

COLD NOODLES

180 g (6½ oz) dried Chinese wheat noodles

1 teaspoon toasted sesame oil

½ Persian (short) cucumber, julienned

2 spring onions (scallions), thinly sliced

handful of coriander (cilantro) leaves, chopped

SESAME DRESSING

3 tablespoons Chinese sesame seed paste

1½ tablespoons soy sauce

1 tablespoon Chilli crisp oil (page 23)

2 teaspoons finely grated fresh ginger

2 teaspoons Chinese black vinegar

2 teaspoons caster (superfine) sugar or honey

1 teaspoon freshly minced garlic

1 teaspoon toasted sesame oil

TO SERVE

2 teaspoons toasted sesame seeds

2 teaspoons crushed roasted salted peanuts (optional)

Chilli crisp oil (page 23)

Cook the noodles according to the packet instructions, then drain, reserving 3 tablespoons of the cooking water, and rinse the noodles under cold water until completely cooled. Drain again.

Place the noodles in a bowl, drizzle with the sesame oil and toss to coat the noodles. Leave in the fridge to chill while preparing the remaining ingredients.

In a large bowl, whisk together the sesame dressing ingredients. Whisk in the reserved warm noodle cooking water, a tablespoon at a time, until the desired consistency is achieved.

Add the chilled noodles to the dressing and toss together well.

Divide the noodles between two serving bowls. Top with the cucumber, spring onion and chopped coriander. Sprinkle with the sesame seeds and crushed peanuts, drizzle with chilli crisp oil and serve immediately.

SERVES 4–6

CHOW MEIN CHICKEN NOODLE SALAD

COLD NOODLES

400 g (14 oz) shredded roasted chicken

150 g (2 cups) shredded green cabbage

150 g (2 cups) shredded red cabbage

180 g (2 cups) bean sprouts

1 large carrot, coarsely grated

2 celery stalks, sliced

3 spring onions (scallions), thinly sliced

1½ large handfuls of coriander (cilantro) leaves

90–135 g (1–1½ cups) store-bought crispy fried chow mein noodles

30 g (¼ cup) toasted flaked almonds

DRESSING

80 ml (⅓ cup) rice wine vinegar

2 tablespoons toasted sesame oil

3 tablespoons soy sauce

2 tablespoons honey

2 tablespoons hoisin sauce

2 tablespoons toasted sesame seeds

1 tablespoon freshly minced ginger

1 teaspoon freshly minced garlic

Place all the dressing ingredients in a bowl and whisk to combine.

Place all the salad ingredients in a large mixing bowl. Add the dressing and toss to combine.

Serve immediately, so the crispy noodles and toasted almonds retain their crunch.

MAKES 10

PRAWN & MANGO RICE PAPER ROLLS

COLD NOODLES

100 g (3½ oz) dried rice vermicelli noodles

10 round rice paper sheets, 22 cm (8¾ in) diameter

15 cooked prawns (shrimp), peeled and deveined, then sliced in half lengthways

1 mango, thinly sliced

1 red bell pepper (capsicum), thinly sliced

1 long cucumber, sliced into thin batons

bunch of coriander (cilantro), leaves picked

½ bunch of mint, leaves picked

2 tablespoons crushed roasted peanuts (optional)

TO SERVE

Peanut chilli sauce (page 22)

Sweet chilli sauce (page 20)

Nam jim sauce (page 22)

Cook the noodles according to the packet instructions. Drain, then rinse under cold water until cool and drain again. Set aside.

To assemble the rolls, briefly dip a rice paper sheet in a large bowl of warm water, then place on a tray or platter.

Place three prawn halves across the middle of the sheet. Next to them, on the side nearest to you, place one-tenth of the noodles. Top the noodles with a few slices of mango, bell pepper and cucumber, along with a few coriander and mint leaves and a sprinkling of crushed peanuts, if using.

Fold the bottom of the rice paper sheet over the filling, tuck in the sides, and continue rolling firmly to enclose the filling. Cover with a clean, slightly damp cloth while assembling the remaining rice paper rolls.

Keep the rolls covered until ready to serve, so they don't dry out. (They are best enjoyed within an hour of rolling.)

Serve the rolls with dipping sauces of your choice.

SERVES 2

KIMCHI BIBIM GUKSU

SPICY COLD NOODLES WITH KIMCHI

COLD NOODLES

220 g (8 oz) dried somyeon (thin wheat noodles)

100 g (⅔ cup) kimchi, chopped

2 × 6-minute jammy Mayak eggs (page 19), halved

10 cherry tomatoes, halved

½ Persian (short) cucumber, julienned

2 teaspoons toasted sesame seeds

crumbled or shredded toasted nori (Korean gim), to serve

SAUCE

2 tablespoons gochujang paste

3 tablespoons kimchi juice

2 tablespoons rice wine vinegar

2 tablespoons caster (superfine) sugar

2 tablespoons soy sauce

1 teaspoon gochugaru chilli powder

1 tablespoon toasted sesame oil

1 garlic clove, minced

Place all the sauce ingredients in a large mixing bowl and whisk to combine. Set aside.

Cook the noodles according to the packet instructions. Drain, rinse under cold water and plunge into an ice water bath to chill completely.

When you're ready to serve, drain the noodles and add them to the sauce along with the kimchi, tossing to coat the noodles completely.

Serve the saucy noodles topped with the egg halves, tomato and cucumber, and finished with a sprinkling of toasted sesame seeds and toasted nori.

SERVES 4

CHA SOBA

COLD GREEN TEA SOBA NOODLE SALAD

400 g (14 oz) dried cha soba noodles (green tea noodles)

bunch of broccolini, trimmed and sliced into thirds

100 g (1 cup) snow peas (mangetout), trimmed

250 g (9 oz) silken tofu, cubed

large handful of watercress, Asian salad greens or mizuna leaves

1 Persian (short) cucumber, julienned

2 radishes, thinly sliced

TO SERVE

Miso ginger dressing (page 21)

1 tablespoon black sesame seeds

2 spring onions (scallions), thinly sliced

Cook the noodles according to the packet instructions. Drain and rinse under cold water, then plunge into an ice water bath to chill completely. Drain again and chill the noodles in the fridge while preparing the salad ingredients and dressing.

Blanch the broccolini in a pot of salted boiling water for 2–3 minutes, or until just tender but still vibrant green. For the last 1½ minutes of cooking, add the snow peas to the boiling water to blanch.

Drain and refresh the vegetables in an ice water bath to stop the cooking process and chill completely. Slice the snow peas in half, or thirds if they are very large.

Divide the chilled noodles among serving bowls. Top with the blanched vegetables, tofu and remaining salad ingredients.

Generously drizzle some miso ginger dressing over the salad, sprinkle with the sesame seeds and spring onion and serve.

SERVES 2

HIYASHI TANUKI UDON

CHILLED UDON NOODLES WITH CRISPY TEMPURA CRUMBS

COLD NOODLES

400 g (14 oz) fresh udon noodles

4 ice cubes

MENTSUYA (COLD BROTH)

400 ml (13½ fl oz) Dashi stock (page 16)

120 ml (4 fl oz) shoyu (Japanese soy sauce)

120 ml (4 fl oz) mirin

2½ tablespoons sake

1 teaspoon caster (superfine) sugar

TO SERVE

3 tablespoons rehydrated wakame (see Note)

7.5–10 cm (3–4 in) piece of daikon, peeled, then spiralised or shaved into ribbons

90 g (½ cup) thinly sliced Persian (short) cucumber

1 large spring onion (scallion), thinly sliced

1 hard-boiled egg, halved

½ toasted nori sheet, shredded

4–6 tablespoons tenkasu (store-bought deep-fried tempura crumbs)

4 teaspoons bonito flakes (katsuobushi)

1½ teaspoons toasted sesame seeds

2 teaspoons wasabi paste, to serve

To make the mentsuya, combine the dashi stock, soy, mirin, sake and sugar in a saucepan over medium–high heat and bring to the boil. Whisk until the sugar has dissolved, then remove from the heat and set aside to cool. Transfer to a clean container, cover and leave in the fridge to chill completely. The mentsuya can be prepared a day ahead.

When ready to serve, cook the noodles according to the packet instructions. Drain and rinse under cold water, then plunge into an ice water bath for a few minutes to chill completely.

Drain the noodles again, then divide between two serving bowls. Pour the chilled mentsuya broth over the noodles and add two ice cubes to each bowl.

Top with the wakame, daikon, cucumber, spring onion, egg halves and nori. Sprinkle with the tenkasu, bonito flakes and sesame seeds and serve straight away, with the wasabi on the side.

Note: You can buy wakame dried or already rehydrated; 1 tablespoon chopped dried wakame = 3 tablespoons rehydrated wakame. To rehydrate dried wakame, cover it with warm water and leave it to soak for 15 minutes, then drain before using.

SAN CHOY BAO

150 g (5½ oz) glass noodles (mung bean vermicelli noodles)

1 teaspoon cornflour (corn starch)

4 teaspoons peanut oil

4 teaspoons toasted sesame oil

3 shallots, finely diced

1 tablespoon freshly minced garlic

1 tablespoon freshly minced ginger

1 carrot, finely diced

125 g (4½ oz) fresh shiitake mushrooms, finely diced

450 g (1 lb) minced (ground) pork

220 g (8 oz) tinned water chestnuts, drained, rinsed and finely diced

3 spring onions (scallions), thinly sliced

SAUCE

60 ml (¼ cup) hoisin sauce

2 tablespoons shaoxing rice wine

2 tablespoons soy sauce

1 tablespoon Chinese black vinegar

1 teaspoon toasted sesame oil

TO SERVE

16 baby cos (romaine) lettuce leaves, washed and patted dry

50 g (⅓ cup) crushed roasted salted peanuts

large handful of coriander (cilantro), roughly chopped

sriracha chilli sauce and/or thinly sliced long red chilli

In a small bowl, whisk together the sauce ingredients. Set aside.

Cook the noodles according to the packet instructions. Drain, then rinse under cold water and drain again. Cut the noodles into smaller lengths using kitchen scissors, then set aside.

In a small bowl, whisk the cornflour with 1 tablespoon of water to form a smooth slurry. Set aside.

Place a wok over high heat. Add the peanut oil and sesame oil. When warmed through, add the shallot, garlic, ginger, carrot and mushrooms. Cook, stirring and tossing, for 2–3 minutes, or until the carrot begins to soften.

Add the pork and cook for 3–4 minutes, or until browned, breaking up the meat with a wooden spoon. Add the water chestnuts and the sauce, stirring to thoroughly coat the meat and vegetables. Cook for another 2 minutes, to allow the mixture to absorb the sauce.

Reduce the heat to medium–low, add the cornflour slurry and stir for a further minute or so, until the mixture has thickened slightly. Finish by tossing through the spring onion, mixing well.

To serve, divide the noodles among the lettuce leaves, then spoon on some of the pork mixture and sprinkle with the peanuts and coriander. Serve with sriracha chilli sauce and/or sliced red chilli on the side.

SERVES 4–6 AS A SIDE

SOM TAM RICE NOODLE SALAD

THAI GREEN PAPAYA SALAD WITH RICE NOODLES

100 g (3½ oz) dried rice vermicelli noodles

2 garlic cloves, peeled

2–4 red bird's eye chillies, to taste, stems removed

1 teaspoon shrimp paste (see Note)

3 tablespoons lime juice

3 tablespoons grated palm sugar

2½–3 tablespoons fish sauce

400 g (14 oz) green papaya, peeled and shredded

2–3 snake (yard-long) beans, cut into 2 cm (¾ in) lengths

100 g (3½ oz) cherry tomatoes, halved, or quartered if large

large handful of bean sprouts

3 tablespoons crushed roasted peanuts

small handful of coriander (cilantro) leaves (optional)

Cook the noodles according to the packet instructions. Drain, then rinse under cold water, drain again and set aside.

Using a large mortar and pestle, pound the garlic, chillies and shrimp paste together into a paste. Add the lime juice, palm sugar and fish sauce and mix to combine.

Add the papaya and snake beans and lightly crush or pound together with the fragrant dressing. Taste, then adjust the balance of flavours, adding more chilli, lime juice, sugar or fish sauce as desired.

Place the noodles in a large serving bowl with the tomato, bean sprouts, peanuts and coriander, if using.

Spoon the fragrant papaya and snake bean mixture over the top and toss well to combine. Serve immediately.

Note: Instead of the shrimp paste, you could use 2 tablespoons dried shrimp, rehydrated in a small amount of water for 5–10 minutes.

SERVES 3

SPICY CUCUMBER NOODLE SALAD

COLD NOODLES

150 g (5½ oz) dried Chinese wheat noodles

3 Persian (short) cucumbers, halved lengthways and sliced into 1 cm (½ in) chunks

handful of roughly chopped coriander (cilantro)

1 tablespoon toasted sesame seeds

3 tablespoons crushed roasted peanuts

DRESSING

3 tablespoons rice wine vinegar

3–4 tablespoons Chilli crisp oil (page 23), to taste

1½ tablespoons light soy sauce

1 tablespoon finely grated ginger

2 teaspoons finely grated garlic

2 teaspoons toasted sesame oil

2 teaspoons honey

Cook the noodles according to the packet instructions. Drain and rinse under cold water until completely cooled, then drain again. Place in a large mixing bowl and set aside.

Place all the dressing ingredients in a small bowl and whisk to combine.

Add the cucumber and dressing to the noodles, tossing thoroughly to coat the noodles. Chill in the fridge for about 10 minutes to allow the flavours to develop.

To serve, toss the coriander, sesame seeds and peanuts through the noodles and divide among serving bowls.

SERVES 2

HIYASHI CHUKA SOMEN

JAPANESE 'CHILLED CHINESE' NOODLES

COLD NOODLES

1 tablespoon vegetable oil

2–3 eggs, beaten

pinch of sea salt

220 g (8 oz) dried somen noodles

4 ham slices, cut into strips

½ Persian (short) cucumber, julienned

1 tomato, cut into wedges, or 8 cherry tomatoes, halved

8 cooked prawns (shrimp), peeled and deveined, tails left intact

benishoga (red pickled ginger), to serve

DRESSING

3 tablespoons soy sauce

2 tablespoons mirin

2 tablespoons Dashi stock (page 16)

1½ tablespoons rice wine vinegar

1 tablespoon toasted sesame oil

1½ teaspoons caster (superfine) sugar

1 teaspoon toasted sesame seeds

1 teaspoon freshly grated ginger

pinch of white pepper

Place the dressing ingredients in a small bowl and whisk to combine. Set aside.

Heat the oil in an omelette pan over medium–high heat. Pour in the beaten egg, swirling the pan to thinly cover the base, and sprinkle with sea salt. Cook for about 1 minute, or until the top of the egg is starting to set, then carefully flip and fry the other side until cooked through. Transfer the omelette to a chopping board, roll it up and slice it into thin strips. Set aside.

Cook the noodles according to the packet instructions. Drain, rinse under cold water, then plunge into an ice water bath for a few minutes to chill completely.

Drain the noodles again and place in a large mixing bowl. Toss the dressing through, coating the noodles well.

Divide the noodles between two plates. Top with the omelette strips, ham, cucumber, tomato and prawns. Serve immediately, with a side of benishoga.

SERVES 3–4

PRAWN & WATERMELON NOODLE SALAD

COLD NOODLES

100 g (3½ oz) dried rice vermicelli noodles

1 tablespoon fish sauce

2 teaspoons caster (superfine) sugar

12 large prawns (shrimp), peeled and deveined, tails left intact

500 g (1 lb 2 oz) watermelon flesh, cut into small wedges (see Note)

200 g (7 oz) cherry tomatoes, halved

2 shallots or ½ small red onion, thinly sliced

1 Persian (short) cucumber, halved lengthways and sliced

large handful each of Vietnamese mint, coriander (cilantro) and mint leaves

50 g (⅓ cup) salted roasted cashews, roughly chopped

TO SERVE

Nam jim sauce (page 22)

2–3 red bird's eye chillies, thinly sliced

lime wedges

Cook the noodles according to the packet instructions. Drain, then rinse under cold water, drain again and set aside on a large serving plate.

Place a small saucepan of water over high heat and bring to the boil. Add the fish sauce and sugar. Add the prawns and poach for 2–3 minutes, or until the prawns have turned pinky-orange in colour and are cooked through.

Drain the prawns, then plunge into an ice water bath to stop the cooking process. When cooled, drain well and arrange on top of the noodles.

Add the remaining salad ingredients to the platter and loosely toss to combine.

Drizzle the nam jim sauce over the salad and serve straight away, with sliced chilli and lime wedges.

Note: You'll need about half a small watermelon for this salad; start with an 800 g (1 lb 12 oz) portion with the skin still on.

INST
NOO

ANT
DLES

SERVES 1

SIZZLING CHILLI NOODLES

INSTANT NOODLES

1 teaspoon finely chopped garlic

1 teaspoon finely chopped fresh ginger

2 spring onions (scallions), thinly sliced

1 small shallot, thinly sliced

1½ teaspoons sesame seeds

1½ teaspoons gochugaru chilli flakes

pinch of red chilli flakes, or to taste

3 tablespoons peanut oil

1½ teaspoons soy sauce

100 g (3½ oz) packet instant ramen noodles, seasoning sachets discarded

TO SERVE

handful of coriander (cilantro) leaves, chopped

large juicy lime wedge

Place the garlic, ginger, spring onion, shallot, sesame seeds and all the chilli flakes in a small heatproof bowl.

Pour the peanut oil into a small saucepan and place over high heat for 1–2 minutes, or until the oil reaches 170°C (335°F) on a cooking thermometer.

Carefully pour the hot oil over the chilli and shallot mixture and let it sizzle. Add the soy sauce and stir to combine.

Cook the noodles according to the packet instructions. Drain and add to the bowl of sizzling chilli oil, mixing well to combine.

Serve, topped with coriander leaves and a juicy lime wedge to squeeze over.

SERVES 1

RAMEN 'MAC N CHEESE'

INSTANT NOODLES

100 g (3½ oz) packet instant ramen noodles, seasoning sachets discarded

CRUNCHY PANKO TOPPING

1 tablespoon salted butter

15 g (¼ cup) panko breadcrumbs

¼ teaspoon garlic powder

pinch of sea salt flakes

1 teaspoon sesame seeds

CHEESY SAUCE

1 teaspoon cornflour (corn starch)

60 ml (¼ cup) milk

60 g (¼ cup) sour cream

1 tablespoon butter

1 teaspoon dijon mustard

1 teaspoon soy sauce

60 g (½ cup) shredded melty four-cheese blend (red cheddar, cheddar, parmesan, mozzarella)

1 slice American burger cheese, chopped

pinch of white pepper

TO SERVE

1 spring onion (scallion), green part only, thinly sliced

sriracha chilli sauce

To make the crunchy panko topping, melt the butter in a small frying pan over medium heat. Add the remaining ingredients and stir for a few minutes, until the panko breadcrumbs and sesame seeds are golden brown and toasty. Set aside.

Cook the noodles according to the packet instructions. Drain, reserving 2–3 tablespoons of the noodle cooking water, and set aside.

To make the cheesy sauce, whisk the cornflour in a small bowl with 1 teaspoon of water to make a smooth slurry. In a saucepan, whisk the milk, sour cream, butter, mustard and soy sauce together over medium heat. Add the cornflour slurry and whisk for 1 minute to thicken slightly. Add the cheeses and whisk until melted, then season with white pepper to taste.

Now add the noodles to the pan and toss well, coating all the strands in the cheesy sauce. Stir in 1–2 tablespoons of the reserved cooking water to thin the sauce if desired.

Serve your mac 'n' cheese ramen in a bowl, sprinkled with the crunchy panko topping, the spring onion greens and a drizzle of sriracha chilli sauce.

SERVES 2

SPICY KIMCHI GOCHUJANG NOODLES

INSTANT NOODLES

200 g (7 oz) dried scissor-cut noodles or 2 × 100 g (3½ oz) packets instant ramen noodles, seasoning sachets discarded

40 g (1½ oz) salted butter

1½ teaspoons caster (superfine) sugar

2 tablespoons gochujang paste

60 g (½ cup) kimchi, chopped

60 ml (¼ cup) kimchi juice

60 ml (¼ cup) chicken stock

TO SERVE

2 egg yolks

2 spring onions (scallions), thinly sliced

small handful of coriander (cilantro) leaves

½ teaspoon black sesame seeds

½ teaspoon toasted white sesame seeds

Chilli crisp oil (page 23)

Cook the noodles according to the packet instructions. Drain, reserving 60 ml (¼ cup) of the noodle cooking water. Rinse the noodles and set aside.

Melt the butter in a wok over medium heat. Add the sugar, gochujang paste and kimchi. Cook for about 2 minutes to slightly caramelise the kimchi, then stir in the kimchi juice and chicken stock. Simmer for a minute or two to reduce slightly.

Add the noodles and toss them through the sauce, coating well. Pour over the reserved noodle cooking water, a tablespoon at a time, to thin the sauce slightly if desired.

Divide the spicy noodles between two serving bowls. Top each with an egg yolk, the spring onion, coriander leaves and sesame seeds. Drizzle with chilli crisp oil and serve, mixing the egg yolk through the noodles.

YAKISOBA PAN

NOODLES IN A HOT DOG BUN

6–8 koppe pan rolls (see Notes)

60 g (¼ cup) kewpie mayonnaise, plus extra for drizzling

2 tablespoons benishoga (red pickled ginger)

1–1½ tablespoons bonito flakes (katsuobushi) or aonori (dried green seaweed)

SAUCE

50 ml (1¾ fl oz) Japanese worcestershire sauce, such as Bulldog (see Notes)

1½ tablespoons oyster sauce

1 tablespoon tomato ketchup

2 teaspoons soy sauce

2 teaspoons sugar

pinch of black pepper

YAKISOBA

2 tablespoons neutral-flavoured vegetable oil

¼ onion, thinly sliced

1 carrot, julienned or grated

55 g (1 cup) thinly sliced wombok (Chinese cabbage)

1 spring onion (scallion), thinly sliced

180 g (6½ oz) instant yakisoba noodles, cooked according to the packet instructions

In a small bowl, whisk together all the sauce ingredients and set aside.

To make the yakisoba, place a wok over high heat, add the oil and warm through. Add the onion and stir-fry for 2–2½ minutes, until translucent. Add the carrot, cabbage and spring onion and quickly toss for another minute or two. Pour in the sauce and toss again to combine with the vegetables. Add the noodles and give it all a final toss, thoroughly coating the noodles and vegetables in the sauce.

Using a sharp knife, split the top of the buns open from one end to the other. Generously spread the mayonnaise inside the buns.

Fill the buns with the yakisoba and add an extra squiggle of mayonnaise across the top. Add the benishoga and a sprinkle of bonito flakes or aonori and enjoy immediately.

Notes: Koppe pan rolls are soft, fluffy split-top hot dog buns made from a brioche dough. Look for them where Japanese baked goods are sold.

If you cannot find Japanese worcestershire sauce, such as the Bulldog brand, substitute with tonkatsu sauce or yakisoba sauce, all found in Asian grocery stores.

SERVES 2

SPICY PEANUT BUTTER NOODLES

INSTANT NOODLES

270 g (9½ oz) instant ramen noodles, seasoning sachets discarded

1 tablespoon chopped garlic chives

2 tablespoons crushed roasted peanuts

lime wedges, to serve

SAUCE

3 tablespoons smooth peanut butter

2 tablespoons gochujang paste

1 tablespoon soy sauce

1½ teaspoons rice wine vinegar

2½ teaspoons coconut sugar or caster (superfine) sugar

1 teaspoon kecap manis or sweet soy sauce

1 teaspoon Chilli crisp oil (page 23), plus extra to serve

Cook the noodles according to the packet instructions. Drain, reserving 3 tablespoons of the noodle cooking water, and set aside.

Combine the sauce ingredients in a bowl and whisk to combine. Mix in 1–2 tablespoons of the noodle cooking water until the desired consistency is achieved.

Add the noodles to the sauce and toss to combine.

Divide between two serving bowls, sprinkle with the garlic chives and peanuts and serve with lime wedges and extra chilli crisp oil.

SERVES 1

FIRECRACKER RAMEN

INSTANT NOODLES

100 g (3½ oz) packet instant ramen noodles, seasoning sachets discarded

15 g (½ oz) butter

60 g (⅔ cup) sliced button mushrooms

1½ teaspoons dark soy sauce

FIRECRACKER SAUCE

1½ teaspoons peanut oil

2 garlic cloves, finely chopped

1½ teaspoons freshly grated ginger

1½ teaspoons Chilli crisp oil (page 23)

1½ teaspoons sriracha chilli sauce

1½ teaspoons gochujang paste

½ teaspoon gochugaru chilli flakes

1½ teaspoons kecap manis

200 ml (7 fl oz) coconut milk

125 ml (½ cup) vegetable stock or water

TO SERVE

1 spring onion (scallion), thinly sliced

coriander (cilantro) leaves

Chilli crisp oil (page 23)

lime wedges

Cook the noodles according to the packet instructions. Drain, rinse and set aside in a serving bowl.

Melt the butter in a small frying pan over medium heat and fry the mushrooms for about 3 minutes, until golden brown and cooked. Splash in the soy sauce, coating the mushrooms thoroughly. Cook for a minute or two, until caramelised. Remove from the heat and set aside.

To make the firecracker sauce, heat the peanut oil in a small saucepan over medium heat and fry the garlic and ginger together for 50–60 seconds, or until fragrant.

Stir in the chilli crisp oil, sriracha chilli sauce, gochujang paste and gochugaru flakes. Sizzle together for 30–40 seconds, then add the kecap manis, coconut milk and stock. Stir to combine, then simmer for a couple of minutes for all the flavours to come together.

Pour the firecracker sauce over the noodles and top with the fried mushrooms. Finish with the spring onion, coriander leaves and a good drizzle of chilli crisp oil and enjoy with lime wedges.

SERVES 2

SICHUAN 'CACIO E PEPE' RAMEN

INSTANT NOODLES

2 teaspoons black peppercorns

1 teaspoon sichuan peppercorns

2 × 100 g (3½ oz) packets instant ramen noodles, seasoning sachets discarded

40 g (1½ oz) butter

1 tablespoon white miso paste (shiro miso)

40 g (1½ oz) freshly grated pecorino

40 g (1½ oz) freshly grated parmesan

In a wok or small frying pan, toast all the peppercorns over medium heat for 30–40 seconds, or until fragrant. Blitz in a spice grinder or lightly crush using a mortar and pestle, then set aside, keeping the wok or pan handy.

Cook the noodles according to the packet instructions. Drain, reserving 250 ml (1 cup) of the noodle cooking water, and set aside.

Melt the butter in the wok or pan over medium–high heat. Add about 2½ teaspoons of the toasted peppercorns, reserving the rest for topping the noodles, and stir together for about 30 seconds.

Add 125 ml (½ cup) of the reserved noodle cooking water and the miso paste. Whisk together until combined, then add the noodles and half the pecorino and parmesan. Toss to coat, reduce the heat to low and add the remaining cheese, tossing and stirring until the noodles are well coated and the sauce is creamy. If needed, add the remaining cooking water, a little at a time, to achieve a lush, creamy sauce.

Divide the noodles between two serving bowls, sprinkle with the remaining toasted crushed peppercorns and enjoy straight away.

SERVES 3–4

KOREAN CHEESY CORN RAMEN

INSTANT NOODLES

240 g (8½ oz) Korean ramyun instant noodles, seasoning sachets discarded

40 g (1½ oz) salted butter

2 garlic cloves, minced

1 teaspoon gochugaru chilli flakes, plus extra to serve

2 tablespoons gochujang paste

400 g (14 oz) tinned corn kernels, drained and rinsed

2 tablespoons kewpie mayonnaise

150 ml (5 fl oz) double (heavy) cream

100 g (⅔ cup) shredded mozzarella

65 g (2¼ oz) grated American cheese

2 spring onions (scallions), thinly sliced, to serve

Cook the noodles according to the packet instructions. Drain, reserving 125 ml (½ cup) of the noodle cooking water, and set aside.

Melt the butter in a frying pan over medium heat and saute the garlic for 30–40 seconds, or until fragrant. Add the chilli flakes and cook, stirring, for another 30–40 seconds. Stir in the gochujang paste and corn until well combined, then cook for about 3 minutes to allow the flavours to meld.

Add the mayonnaise and cream to the corn mixture and simmer for 2–3 minutes, until creamy. Add the cooked noodles and 60 ml (¼ cup) of the warm reserved noodle cooking water, stirring to combine.

Now stir both the cheeses through, along with a little more of the reserved noodle water, until your desired level of sauciness is achieved.

Reduce the heat to low, cover with a lid, and allow the cheese to melt thoroughly for another minute or so.

Serve immediately, with a scattering of spring onion and extra gochugaru chilli flakes.

SERVES 2

ZARU SOBA

QUICK COLD SOBA NOODLES

200 g (7 oz) dried soba noodles

3 tablespoons shredded toasted nori

2 small ice cubes

1 spring onion (scallion), thinly sliced

2 teaspoons toasted sesame seeds

2 teaspoons freshly grated wasabi (see Note)

DIPPING SAUCE

375 ml (1½ cups) Dashi stock (page 16)

120 ml (4 fl oz) shoyu (Japanese soy sauce)

120 ml (4 fl oz) mirin

2½ tablespoons sake

2 teaspoons caster (superfine) sugar

To make the dipping sauce, combine the dashi stock, soy sauce, mirin, sake and sugar in a small saucepan over medium–high heat and bring to the boil. Whisk until the sugar has dissolved, then remove from the heat. Allow to cool, then transfer to a container and leave in the fridge to chill completely. The dipping sauce can be prepared a day ahead.

Cook the noodles according to the packet instructions. Drain, rinse under cold water until completely cold, then drain again.

Divide the noodles between two bamboo serving mats or bowls and top with a sprinkling of nori.

Pour the dipping sauce into two serving bowls. Add an ice cube to each one and mix in the spring onion, sesame seeds and wasabi.

Use chopsticks to dip the noodles into the sauce before taking a bite.

Note: If you can't get fresh wasabi, you can use 1 teaspoon wasabi paste or 2 teaspoons freshly grated daikon or radish.

SERVES 1

BUFFALO WING RAMEN

INSTANT NOODLES

100 g (3½ oz) packet chicken-flavoured instant ramen noodles

3 tablespoons sour cream

3 tablespoons hot sauce (such as Frank's Hot sauce), or to taste

15 g (½ oz) salted butter, melted

¼ teaspoon garlic powder

75 g (½ cup) shredded roast chicken

TO SERVE

½ spring onion (scallion), green part only, thinly sliced

a few tender celery leaves

1 tablespoon Blue Cheese Crumbles (see Note) or crumbled blue cheese

hot sauce

Cook the noodles according to the packet instructions, using the chicken-flavoured seasoning.

Meanwhile, combine the sour cream, hot sauce, butter and garlic powder in a small bowl and whisk to combine.

Drain the cooked noodles, reserving 1–2 tablespoons of the noodle cooking water.

Add the noodles to the creamy sauce, mixing well. For a slightly thinner sauce, add a little of the cooking water as desired, tossing to combine.

Toss the chicken through the noodles and top with the spring onion, celery leaves and blue cheese crumbles.

Enjoy straight away, with extra hot sauce on the side.

Note: Blue Cheese Crumbles can be found in the refrigerated section at the supermarket.

SERVES 1

HOT & SPICY CHEESY RAMEN

INSTANT NOODLES

120 g (4½ oz) packet Gourmet Spicy Shin Ramyun Noodles; reserve the spicy seasoning sachet, but discard the vegetable seasoning pack

1½ tablespoons kewpie mayonnaise

1½ tablespoons gochujang paste

1 egg yolk

2 teaspoons freshly minced garlic

pinch of sea salt

35 g (⅓ cup) very finely grated parmesan (see Note), plus extra to serve

1–2 tablespoons chopped garlic chives

Cook the noodles according to the packet instructions.

Meanwhile, empty the spicy seasoning sachet from the noodle packet into a mixing bowl. Add the mayonnaise, gochujang paste, egg yolk, garlic, sea salt and parmesan and whisk to combine.

Drain the cooked noodles, reserving 2–3 tablespoons of the noodle cooking water.

Add the noodles to the bowl of seasoning sauce and toss to coat, stirring in 2–3 tablespoons of the cooking water to make the sauce as creamy and lush as desired.

Tip the noodles into a serving bowl, sprinkle with garlic chives and extra parmesan and enjoy.

Note: If possible, use a microplane to grate the parmesan to give a very fine dusting of cheese that melts easily and smoothly into the sauce.

ABC

一番搾り

SERVES 2

CARBONARA RAMEN

INSTANT NOODLES

1 egg

2 egg yolks

50–60 g (1 cup) very finely grated pecorino romano (see Note), plus extra to serve

1 teaspoon white miso paste (shiro miso)

2 × 100 g (3½ oz) packets instant ramen noodles, seasoning sachets discarded

1 tablespoon olive oil

80 g (2¾ oz) pancetta or bacon, diced

2 garlic cloves, minced

cracked black pepper, to taste

In a small bowl, whisk together the egg, egg yolks, pecorino and miso paste. Set aside.

Cook the noodles according to the packet instructions. Drain, reserving 80 ml (⅓ cup) of the noodle cooking water, and set aside.

Heat the olive oil in a wok or small frying pan over medium heat and fry the pancetta for about 3 minutes, until golden and crispy. Add the garlic and quickly toss through until fragrant, about 30–40 seconds.

Toss the noodles through the pancetta mixture and remove from the heat.

Pour in the beaten egg mixture, tossing well to evenly coat the noodles. Stir in the reserved noodle cooking water a little at a time, until you achieve your desired level of creaminess.

Season well with cracked black pepper, to taste, and toss to combine.

Divide the noodles between two serving bowls, sprinkle with extra pecorino and enjoy straight away.

Note: If possible, use a microplane to grate the pecorino, to give a very fine dusting of cheese that melts easily and smoothly into the sauce.

SERVES 1

EVERYTHING BUT THE BAGEL RAMEN

INSTANT NOODLES

100 g (3½ oz) packet instant ramen noodles, seasoning sachets discarded

2 large eggs

1 tablespoon peanut oil

40 g (1½ oz) unsalted butter

1 teaspoon freshly minced garlic

¼ teaspoon chilli flakes, or to taste

1½ teaspoons brown sugar

4 teaspoons soy sauce

1 spring onion (scallion), thinly sliced

SEASONING

3 tablespoons toasted white sesame seeds

2 tablespoons black sesame seeds

2 tablespoons dried onion flakes

1 tablespoon dried garlic granules

2 teaspoons poppy seeds

2 teaspoons sea salt flakes

Place all the seasoning ingredients in a clean glass jar, secure the lid and shake to combine. You'll have more seasoning than you need for this recipe; the seasoning will keep in the pantry for up to 3 months.

Cook the noodles according to the packet instructions. Drain, reserving 2–3 tablespoons of the noodle cooking water, and set aside.

While the noodles are cooking, beat one of the eggs in a small bowl and set aside.

Place a wok or small frying pan over high heat. Add the peanut oil and when shimmering hot, crack the remaining egg into it and cook for a few minutes, until fried to your liking. Remove the fried egg from the pan and keep warm.

Reduce the heat to medium and add 25 g (1 oz) of the butter to the wok or pan, along with the garlic and chilli flakes. Cook, stirring, for about 30–40 seconds, until the garlic is fragrant.

Stir in the sugar and soy sauce until combined, then add the noodles, tossing to coat them in the sauce and adding 1–2 tablespoons of the reserved noodle cooking water, until your desired level of sauciness is achieved.

Push the noodles to the side of the pan and add the remaining 15 g (½ oz) of butter, allowing it to melt. Add the beaten egg and stir back and forth until scrambled, then combine with the noodles.

Sprinkle with 2–3 teaspoons of the seasoning and toss again to combine.

Tip the noodles into a serving bowl. Top with the fried egg and the spring onion. Sprinkle with more seasoning and enjoy.

SERVES 2

GARLIC BUTTER MISO RAMEN

INSTANT NOODLES

2 × 100 g (3½ oz) packets instant ramen noodles, seasoning sachets discarded

60 g (¼ cup) unsalted butter

2 tablespoons freshly minced garlic

2 tablespoons shoyu (Japanese soy sauce), tamari or soy sauce

1⅓ tablespoons white miso paste (shiro miso)

25 g (¼ cup) very finely grated parmesan, plus extra to serve

1 toasted nori sheet, crumbled, to serve

Cook the noodles according to the packet instructions. Drain, reserving 125 ml (½ cup) of the noodle cooking water, and set aside.

While the noodles are cooking, melt the butter in a wok or frying pan over medium–low heat. Add the garlic and cook, stirring, for 30–40 seconds, until lightly golden and fragrant. Whisk in the shoyu and miso paste until incorporated.

Add the reserved noodle cooking water and whisk to emulsify, creating a buttery, umami sauce.

Now add the noodles to the wok or pan and toss to coat. Sprinkle the parmesan over the top and toss until the cheese has melted.

Divide the noodles between two serving bowls, sprinkle with the nori and a little more parmesan and enjoy.

UNI-EAGLE

SERVES 1–2

RAMEN CHEESY DOG OMELETTE

INSTANT NOODLES

100 g (3½ oz) packet instant spicy chicken-flavoured ramen noodles

1 tablespoon peanut oil or vegetable oil

1 hot dog, sliced into 5 mm (¼ in) thick rounds

3 large eggs

pinch of sea salt

pinch of white pepper

50 g (1¾ oz) grated cheddar or mozzarella

1 spring onion (scallion), thinly sliced

TO SERVE

kewpie mayonnaise

sriracha chilli sauce or Chilli crisp oil (page 23)

furikake

Cook the noodles according to the packet instructions, along with the seasoning sachets provided. Drain and set aside.

While the noodles are cooking, add the peanut oil to an omelette pan set over medium heat. Cook the hot dog slices for about 1 minute on each side, or until seared and golden. Remove from the pan, keeping the pan handy, and set aside.

Beat the eggs in a bowl, season with the salt and white pepper, then pour the egg into the omelette pan and increase the heat to medium–high. Cook the egg, undisturbed, for 50–60 seconds, then add the drained noodles, spreading them evenly across the egg. Top with the grated cheese, spring onion and the fried hot dog slices.

Continue to cook for another minute or so, until the bottom of the omelette has fully set, then fold the omelette in half, covering the cheesy noodles.

Slide the noodle omelette out of the pan and onto a serving plate. Finish with a drizzle of mayonnaise, sriracha chilli sauce or chilli crisp oil and a sprinkling of furikake and enjoy straight away.

INDEX

T

U

V

W

Y

Z

Smith Street Books

Published in 2026 by Smith Street Books
Naarm (Melbourne) | Australia
smithstreetbooks.com

Distributed outside of ANZ, North & Latin America by
Thames & Hudson Ltd., 6–24 Britannia Street, London, WC1X 9JD
thamesandhudson.com

EU Authorised Representative: Interart S.A.R.L.
19 rue Charles Auray, 93500 Pantin, Paris, France
productsafety@thameshudson.co.uk; www.interart.fr

ISBN: 978-1-9235-0318-2

Smith Street Books respectfully acknowledges the Wurundjeri People of the Kulin Nation, who are the Traditional Owners of the land on which we work, and we pay our respects to their Elders past and present.

Publisher: Paul McNally
Managing editor: Lucy Heaver
Editor: Katri Hilden
Recipes: Deborah Kaloper
Additional text: Jane Price
Designer & illustrator: George Saad
Typesetter: Nikola Roberts
Photographer: Daniel Herrmann-Zoll
Food stylist: Deborah Kaloper
Food preparation: Caroline Griffiths & Claire Pietersen
Proofreader: Martine Lleonart
Indexer: Helena Holmgren
Production manager: Aisling Coughlan

Printed & bound in China by C&C Offset Printing Co., Ltd.

Book 469
10 9 8 7 6 5 4 3 2 1

FSC www.fsc.org
MIX
Paper | Supporting responsible forestry
FSC® C008047